YOU MIGHT HAVE ASKED...

Stuart Olyott

 EVANGELICAL PRESS

EVANGELICAL PRESS
16/18 High Street, Welwyn, Hertfordshire, AL6 9EQ, England

© Evangelical Press 1983

First published 1983
Second impression 1987

ISBN 0 85234 175 X

Printed in Great Britain by The Bath Press, Avon

To

Alex and Karen
Joe and Cath
Eric and Pauline
Neil and Brenda
Chris
Wes
Mark
Bernie

'Wisdom is supreme; therefore get wisdom.
Though it cost all you have, get understanding'
(Proverbs 4:7, NIV).

Contents

Preface

Many people planning to climb Snowdon by means of the Pyg track have difficulty in finding exactly where the path starts. Now a rough sign, painted on a rock, makes it clear.

This book is like that sign — it is brief and unsophisticated! It does not tell you about every turn and slope on the path to faith, but simply where to begin. It is a starting-point.

Those who want additional signposts on their way should refer to the titles mentioned at the end of the chapter whose subject they want clarified. In most cases, the first book mentioned is fairly easy reading. The next is not quite so straightforward, but covers more ground. The third requires a little more effort to understand, and may border on the difficult.

Every title mentioned is still in print, and your local Christian bookshop will be pleased to order any of them for you.

Bon voyage!

STUART OLYOTT
Église Evangélique Baptiste,
Lausanne.
1983.

1.
Can we be sure that God exists?

No proof
Everybody knows that the existence of God cannot
be proved.

Of course, ever since the days of Aquinas (1225–
1274) there have been people who have tried to prove
it, and the 'five ways' (five supposed proofs) are
known world-wide. But people who use proofs are
seldom convinced by them themselves. Their own
experience should show them the folly of using
them. Their own faith is not built on them, so why
should they expect other people to come to faith
that way?

Some of these so-called 'proofs' argue from effect
to cause. The universe has come from somewhere, it
is argued, and its existence drives us to the idea of
God. Other arguments are based on the idea of
design in the universe. It is said that there are evidences of design, and so there must be a Designer.

Another argument is the famous 'ontological argument', first used by Anselm (1033–1109), which
argues from the *idea* of God to the *fact* of God.
Like all the 'proofs', it can easily be shot down,
and over the centuries all sorts of folk have taken
great delight in doing so. Once they have demolished
the arguments, the shooters go home thinking that
they have got rid of the Christian faith once and for
all.

But they have not! Bible-believing Christians have
no interest in these 'proofs', and are as good shots

1

as anyone else when it comes to destroying them. At no point does the Christian faith depend on God's existence being proved! People who think it does are very greatly mistaken. They could not be more wrong.

It is reasonable to believe in God

Yet although there is no proof for the existence of God, we must not think that it is irrational or unreasonable to believe in him. We do not have to commit intellectual suicide to be Christians. The Christian faith does not deaden or destroy the mind, or cause people, ostrich-like, to bury their heads in the sands of obscurantism. The scoffing caricatures of Christians which we sometimes meet bear no resemblance to the truth. People who believe in God do not have their eyes closed to the facts. The opposite is true. It is with their eyes wide open to the facts that they try to live for God in this modern world.

Let us think about the universe we are in. It exists, does it not? Did *we* make it? No. So we live in a world which is not of our making — a world which is a highly complex machine or organism, where one slight shift in nature affects the balance of the whole.

What are we to make of this world? Is it the product of blind chance, where everything that happens does so without rhyme or reason? If that is so, we are making reasoned and rational observations in an unreasoned and irrational world! Is that possible?

Does it not make *better* sense of the world, and our thought about it, and our behaviour in it, if we believe what the Bible says? The Bible declares that the universe exists because God created it. The whole thing is now greatly spoiled, but the elements of balance and order which remain reflect the mind of its Creator. Man has his ability to reason and to make judgements because this was a faculty given uniquely to him by him who made all things.

None of this can we prove, of course. But it is nonsense to believe that rational thoughts can arise in an irrational world. By assuming that God exists, and that what the Bible teaches about his creation of the universe and of man is true, we make better sense of the facts which stare us in the face. The uniformity in nature which allows us to formulate physical laws also now makes sense. So does rational man. But what sense does the whole thing make if we *rule out* God?

What about the things which we are going to mention now? Did they just 'happen'? Surely they make better sense if we adopt Christian presuppositions, and believe the Bible's teaching.

Take, for example, what is commonly called 'God-thirst'. Every person has a view of God, even if it is only the negative opinion that he does not exist. Such people are the exceptions, to the point that we have to invent a word to describe them. We have no widely used word for those who believe in a god, because wherever man is found, he is religious. His religions differ vastly, and yet in all of them there are some common elements. All religions have some form of prayer, and usually some teaching about sacrifice. They have regulations about giving to the deity concerned, about formal acts of worship, about daily behaviour and about death and what is beyond it. These unquestioned facts leave a lot of questions to be answered. Why is man religious at all? Why is he universally religious? How is it that there are these common elements in all religions? Why, within these common elements, is there such diversity and contradiction?

A thousand answers have been offered to each of these questions. The answers may have convinced those who put them forward, but have seldom convinced more than a few others. Hardly anybody has attempted to answer *all* the questions above. At the end of the day most men and women simply answer, 'We do not know,' to each one of them. Religion is a fact of man's existence for which he has no convincing explanation.

Yet all the time the Bible speaks plainly to these questions. It tells us that man is religious because he was made originally to enjoy God, on whom he has now walked out. He is universally religious because his rebellion has not meant that he can entirely shake off the sense of the eternal which is built into him. He has a sense of God which will not go away. We *know* that there is a Person who is the author of our existence, and to whom we are answerable. We even know that he is eternal and powerful. To seek to quieten its conscience, our race has invented its own religion, and all religions are degraded forms of an early attempt to placate God by earning his favour. This explains their common elements, whereas man's insistence on worshipping as *he* pleases also explains the diversity which has arisen.

So we look across the world, and see that the Bible gives a reasonable and coherent explanation of one of the great facts of life, where every other explanation has proved bankrupt. The Bible's explanation makes good sense of the facts. When the same book speaks about the infinite-personal God who is the true God, is it unreasonable to believe what it says in *that* area? Its explanation of what we can *see* is reasonable enough. Why should it be thought unreasonable to believe what it says about what we *cannot see*?

Using our minds

Let us extend this argument to another area, and talk about conscience. Man has within him a sense of 'ought'. People lobby governments because certain things 'ought' to be done, and placard and protest about what 'ought not' to have been done. The sense of 'ought' is not the same within every person, but it *is there* within every person, none the less! What is the explanation for this? Where did this sense of 'ought' come from? Did it just 'happen' as we are so often led to believe?

It undoubtedly makes good sense of the facts to accept what the Bible teaches on this question. It tells us that man was created with a sense of moral obligation, having been made in the image of God. Since man's rebellion this image has been defaced, but it has not been removed entirely. The sense of moral obligation remains, but it is distorted. This explains why it is there, but why it does not take the same direction in every individual. Such teaching is reasonable, and perfectly in tune with what we see about us. If the Bible's teaching proves so reasonable in an area that we can observe, why must we assume that it is unreasonable in what it says about an area which we *cannot* observe? Is it not perfectly reasonable to accept what it says about the existence of God?

The sense of 'ought' in man tells him that certain things are 'right', while others are 'wrong'. Each person admits that it is the 'right' which 'ought' to be done, but, when it suits him, he does the 'wrong'! Why do all people everywhere fly in the face of their own conscience, while still admitting that what they

are doing 'ought not' to be done? And why is it that
in certain areas every conscience agrees about what is
right and wrong? People everywhere resent others
insulting their parents, seek to defend themselves
and their loved ones when their lives are threatened,
are furious when their marriage partners yield to the
advances of others, try to track down those who have
stolen their property, object when somebody lies to
them and dislike intensely the thought that somebody else has set his heart on what they themselves
own.

Quite clearly the following laws are written on the
human heart: 'Honour your father and your mother...
You shall not murder. You shall not commit adultery. You shall not steal. You shall not bear false
witness against your neighbour. You shall not covet...
anything that belongs to your neighbour' (Exodus
20:12—17). What is the explanation?

The explanation which the Bible gives is perfectly
reasonable and fits all the observable facts. It teaches
that God's law is a reflection of his own character,
and that when he made man, he wrote his law on
man's heart. Man, constitutionally, has an inbuilt
sense of the law of God — a law which was later
summarized and written as the Ten Commandments.
Man is now in rebellion against God, and his nature
is perverted by sin. He freely disobeys God's law, and
yet his sense of right and wrong remains. His own
convenience now matters more to him than God's
absolutes. But he cannot entirely rid himself of what
God has written within his conscience on the subjects
of parental honour, murder, adultery, stealing, lying
and coveting. The Bible coherently explains the
world *as we see it actually to be.* Why should we
conclude that it is misleading us when it tells us
about God?

A look at man

Let us now look more deeply at man as we find him on this planet. We find a creature which has rationality, a sense of purpose and a fear of non-being. He longs for significance and places great value on the lives of his fellow human beings. He is a genius, as his achievements in science and medicine eloquently testify — as do his skills in designing impressive buildings and in painting beautiful pictures. He has many commendable qualities, such as love, tenderness, loyalty, devotion and self-sacrifice. Yet the very same creature will hurt his fellow with theft, adultery and murder. The genius is also a beast who is capable of inventing concentration camps and weapons well able to blow his world to pieces.

What an enigma man is! Is he just 'time plus chance', as many modern thinkers say? Is he just a random selection of atoms? Or is he what the Bible says he is?

Why should a random selection of atoms long for significance, and be afraid of non-being? Why should a machine which is merely 'time plus chance' place such value on its own kind? If man is a mere machine, how are we to explain the 'spiritual' side of him, which designs and executes such beauty? Why is man a genius above all other creatures? How do we explain the acts of self-sacrifice and the barbarous atrocities found not only in the same race, but often in the same person?

Only the Bible explains man adequately, and gives us a picture of man which exactly tallies with what we see. It tells us that he is the highest creation of God, and was created to have fellowship with him. He was made after God's image. This explains the personal and intellectual qualities which we mentioned first. Yet his whole nature has become perverted, and he now loves himself more than anything else, even more than the God to whom he owes his life. This explains the selfish and spiteful characteristics which we mentioned.

The Bible gives us an absolutely accurate description of man, and makes excellent sense of him. There is no tension between what it teaches about him, and what we actually see him to be. The explanation is full, coherent and convincing. This being so, why should we then throw out the Bible's teaching on God, which runs side by side with this teaching? There is nothing unreasonable about its explanation of man, so why should its teaching on God be thought to be unreasonable?

The map and the jigsaw

To illustrate all this, let us assume that you decide to pay a visit to Belvidere Road Church, Liverpool, where I am sitting as I write this. You decide to come by train, and ring up to find out how to get from the station to the church. In due course we send you a map, but it is never needed, because we pick you up at the station. You get into the car without so much as ever looking at it.

As you are driven along you pass in turn a large hotel, a burnt-out church, the Anglican cathedral, a public library and a police station. These are all prominent buildings and you cannot help noticing them. After our meeting with you we run you back to the station, and you see them all again — this time in reverse order.

While travelling home on the train, you put your hands in your pocket or bag and rediscover the map which we sent to you, and which you have never used. You open it up and see that, on the route which we marked from the station to our church, you were to pass a large hotel, a burnt-out church, the Anglican cathedral, a public library and a police station. You remember having seen all these things, and know that what the map is telling you tallies perfectly with the way things are.

However, as you examine the map more closely, you notice that there is another route from the station to our church. On this route the landmarks indicated are a concert hall, a women's hospital, a synagogue and a picturesque boulevard. This was not the route that you took, and you never saw them. But you do not doubt that they exist. The map was perfectly accurate in the areas where you were able to check up on it, so why should you doubt it when it tells you about things that you have *not* seen?

In the same way, the Bible is perfectly accurate in its description of human religion, the human conscience and all the other areas which this chapter has mentioned. In every area where it can be checked up on, it describes things *as they are*. It does not mislead us in any way, but tells us the truth. On what grounds, then, should we doubt it when it speaks to us about what we *cannot* check up on? Why should we assume that it is misleading us when it tells us about the existence of God?

Imagine that your house has an attic, and that in that attic you find the pieces of a jigsaw. You put them together, but there are only enough of them to make half a picture. The other half of the jigsaw is completely missing. You wonder what picture it gives, and decide to search for the appropriate pieces.

In doing so you come across the lid of a cardboard box. There is a picture on it, and immediately all your questions about the picture on the

missing half of the puzzle are answered. The picture
on the box is the complete picture of the jigsaw
puzzle. You know it is, because the half of the jigsaw that you have completed exactly matches half
of the picture on the box. You rightly assume that
the pieces which you do *not* have, if put together,
would exactly tally with the other half of the picture.
It is not an unreasonable conclusion. There is no
proof for your assumption. But it does not matter
to you. You are completely sure that you know
what the missing half of the puzzle is like.

As we look across the world, we build up, by
observation, a picture of man. The picture we put
together exactly tallies with what the Bible tells us
about him. But we do not have the pieces to put
together a picture of God. We do not know what
he is like. When we turn to the Bible our guessing
is over. Because its teaching about man exactly
tallies with what we can see, we do not question
that its picture about God is also exactly accurate,
although that is a truth which we cannot see for
ourselves. We have no *proof* that its picture is right,
but it is not an unreasonable assumption. Our uncertainty is over, and our doubts are settled. We are
absolutely sure that God *is*, and that the God, who
is, is the God of the Bible. We have arrived at
certainty without proof. But we have not arrived
there without the Bible!

But is it possible that we are putting too much
weight on the Bible? Is it really as trustworthy as
we claim? If it is, why are there so many people who
suspect it, and even attack it? Such questions as
these are beyond the scope of this present chapter,
but we will face each one of them in the next.

Knowing God

Before we come to the next chapter, there is a further point that should be made here. It is one thing to know the truth about God. It is quite another to know him for ourselves.

The Bible assures us of the existence of God, and tells us what he is like. It gives us information about his essential nature, about his attributes and about his character. It records how he has revealed himself in history, and unveils something of his eternal purposes. It states what are his promises, and what are his threats. We are told a new fact about him on almost every page.

One of the things we are told is that this God may be *known*. He is not a *something* which we cannot describe, but a *Someone*. God is a personal Spirit. He has names. He has communication with men and women, and more than one has become known as his 'friend' (Exodus 33:11; James 2:23). The central message of the Scriptures is to explain how those who are alienated from him can walk with him again.

The Bible warns us not to be satisfied with simply knowing that God exists. Nor are we to be content if we can relate everything which he has revealed about himself. It encourages us to seek him — and to keep seeking him until we *find* him.

From time to time I have met people who are great admirers of the queen. They seem to know everything about her. They know when and where she was born, what are her interests, and what she prefers to eat. There seems to be no question about her which they cannot answer. Yet all their knowledge has come to them from library books and magazine articles. They have never met the queen for themselves — not so much as on one of her famous 'walkabouts'!

God is willing to be known. This is the real reason he has revealed himself. But he is not content that we should simply have accurate information about him. He wants us to come to the place where he is no longer a stranger to us, and where we love him with all our heart and soul (Matthew 22:37).

This is somewhere where he himself must bring us. Recently I was speaking to an acknowledged intellectual who had spent nearly forty years as an outspoken atheist. He confessed to me that during that period he had occasional moments where his conscience convinced him that God existed, although his considerable intellect frankly contradicted this. One such moment threw him into complete turmoil, and he determined that he would reopen the whole question of the existence of God in his thinking.

He said that he felt conscious that God existed, and yet could not be convinced intellectually. In genuine distress at the enigma of his position, he decided to pray in the following terms: 'O God, I do not, at this moment, actually believe in you. But if you *are* there, it must be you who finds me — for I am completely unable to find you on my own.'

It was very shortly afterwards that he turned to the Scriptures, and was completely convinced by what he read there. Not long after that he came into the personal experience of knowing God of which the Bible so often speaks. His sharp mind and literary gifts are now used in expounding the Christian faith and applying its teachings to this modern world.

But is it possible that his confidence in the Scriptures is misplaced? The time to consider this question has now come.

To pursue this subject:

    *Why I believe in God by Cornelius Van Til. (Booklet, Presbyterian and Reformed Publishing Company.)
   **The Everlasting God by David Broughton Knox. (Paperback, Evangelical Press.)
  ***Christian Theistic Evidences by Cornelius Van Til. (Paperback, Presbyterian and Reformed Publishing Company.)

2.
Can the Bible be trusted?

The Bible is a collection of sixty-six separate books written between 1500 B.C. and 100 A.D. by about forty authors who claimed divine inspiration. It is the most widely circulated book of all time, and it is currently available, in whole or in part, in over 1,600 languages and dialects.

The first thirty-nine books of the Bible are known as the 'Old Testament', and they trace the purposes of God from creation to four hundred years before Christ, whose coming they repeatedly predict. Mostly written in Hebrew, the Old Testament contains three sorts of literature — history, poetry and prophecy.

The last twenty-seven books are known as the 'New Testament', and this title is intended to convey that the books contain the fulfilment of what the Old Testament promised. Written in Greek, the New Testament has four divisions: four Gospels, the Acts of the Apostles, the Epistles (or letters) and the Revelation. It covers a period from just before the birth of Christ to the spread of the Christian message throughout the Roman Empire.

What Christians believe about the Bible can best be summarized in an anonymous paragraph which is sometimes found printed at the front of Bibles intended for free distribution: 'This book contains the mind of God, the state of man, the way of salvation, the doom of sinners and the happiness of believers. Its doctrines are holy, its precepts are binding, its histories are true and its decisions are immutable. Read it to be wise, believe it to be saved

and practise it to be holy. It contains light to direct
you, food to support you and comfort to cheer you.
It is the traveller's map, the pilot's compass, the
soldier's sword and the Christian's charter. Here
paradise is restored, Heaven opened, and the gates of
hell disclosed. Christ is its grand subject, our good
its design, and the glory of God its end. Read it
slowly, frequently, prayerfully. It is a mine of wealth,
a paradise of glory and a river of pleasure. It will
reward the greatest labour and condemn all who
trifle with its sacred contents. It is the Book of
books — God's book — the revelation of God to
man.'

But is all this true? Is it possible that the great
confidence that Christians have in the Bible is misplaced? Why are they so sure that this book is
nothing less than the Word of God to his world?

No book like it
The first reason why Christians trust the Bible is
because, frankly, there is no other book like it in
the world. It is in a class of its own. It is unique.
Let us note some of the features which make it
different from every other book which has ever
been written.

Its prophecies come true. We could give many
examples of this. We could survey what Ezekiel wrote
in 590 B.C. about the future of Tyre, and how this
was exactly fulfilled in subsequent history (see
Ezekiel chapter 26). Micah predicted the future of
Samaria, Zephaniah the future of Gaza and Ashkelon,
and Isaiah and Jeremiah the future of Babylon.
Daniel accurately predicted the three great empires
which would dominate world affairs for the five
centuries after his lifetime, and Jesus vividly described the destruction of Jerusalem forty years

before it took place. All these prophecies can be dated, and their accuracy checked out by a comparison with what later occurred. There is no possibility of a fake, and we have to come up with an explanation. The writers themselves claim that the true Author of their prophecies was God!

Of particular importance are the Old Testament prophecies concerning the coming Messiah. Bethlehem is predicted as the city of his birth, Galilee as the sphere of his labours and Jerusalem as the place of his death. The details of his death are particularly specific, and it was the reading of Psalm 22 and Isaiah chapter 53 which finally settled my own doubts and brought me to embrace the Bible as being a book of supernatural origin and divine inspiration. There are over five hundred prophecies regarding Christ in the Old Testament, and all of them are known to have been penned and in circulation over four hundred years before his birth. There is no other book in the world with such a record!

It is sixty-six books, yet it speaks as one book. The forty writers of the books of the Bible were very different from each other. They varied in social position, from royalty to peasant. Some were educated men of letters, one was a physician and others wrote in a jarring and rugged style which betrayed their lack of schooling. While all but one were Jews, it must be remembered that they lived and wrote in different countries and were often separated from each other by a span of centuries. The deaths of Moses and the apostle John were actually 1600 years apart! From the pens of these writers came history, biography, apocalyptic, theology, philosophy and pithy maxims of practical advice. No two wrote in the same style and vocabulary, and the vast majority never met each other, or had any other form of contact.

But all this diversity has not affected the unity of the Bible. Impartial readers are staggered to discover how each writer's work complements the others, and how the whole book is without any contradictions. The Bible is marked with a marvellous harmony, and the many authors are in perfect agreement about the existence and character of God, the person and work of Christ, the nature of sin, the definition of righteousness, the certainty of judgement, the bliss of heaven, the punishment of hell — and every other doctrine and theme which they cover. Such agreement is nothing less than astonishing, and Christians believe that it can only be explained by concluding that all the authors wrote under the same inspiration, and that their writings are nothing other than the Word of God.

It teaches truths beyond our human understanding. The penmen of the Bible were human, as we have just seen. Yet it is a fact that they penned concepts which no human has yet been able to grasp and understand! How can a man invent and write down things which neither he nor others can comprehend? It is impossible. If it was only an isolated incident, we might brush it aside. But it was not. Writer after writer wrote down the same incomprehensible concepts, complementing what others had written on the same subject, but never compromising or contradicting it. We can only conclude that such writers received their concepts from a higher source, and this is, in fact, what each of them claimed. They constantly asserted that their words were given to them by God.

What are some of these incomprehensible themes? We can define *what* the Bible says in these areas but cannot understand *how* these things can be. What does it really mean for God to be *eternal* — without

beginning, without end, of infinite years and yet
beyond and above time? Can the human mind
imagine how he, simply by speaking, made all things
of *nothing*? How can it be that this God is one in
his essential being, and yet that there are *three* who
are God — without there being three gods? How
could God the Son continue to be what he always
was (God), and yet become what he previously was
not (man)? How was it possible for him to be born
of a sinner, and yet to be sinless? How do we plumb
the mystery of his person, that he is fully God,
fully man and yet only one Christ? The majesty of
what the Bible teaches perplexes us, especially when
we see such high themes couched in simple and
straightforward terms. It overwhelms us, and all our
consciences testify that we are faced with nothing
less than the truth of the living God.

It has withstood all attacks. The history of the
Bible is enough to convince the impartial observer
that it enjoys nothing less than divine protection. No
ancient book is well preserved, because the mistakes
of generations of copyists have meant that we cannot
be totally certain of the original text of any of them.
In addition to this difficulty, the Bible was banned
or burned by antagonistic authorities and severely
mutilated and altered by heretics. Despite all this, it
stands as the best preserved book of all time, and the
sifting disciplines of textual critics mean that there
are only about sixty words in it of which we are
uncertain — and none of these affects the meaning
of any vital passage or our understanding of any
biblical doctrine or theme. What force has been at
work in history to protect this book in this unique
manner? Why should *this* book alone, of all ancient
books, have enjoyed such protection?

The French atheistic philosopher Voltaire (1694—

1778) scoffed at the Bible, and predicted that en-
lightened mankind would soon stop reading it. Two
hundred years after his death the Bible is more
widely read than ever — but who reads Voltaire?
Millions of pounds have been spent in attempts to
discredit the Bible, and all of them have failed. Some
of those funded to engage in this destructive research
have actually been turned round by their studies
and have become outspoken advocates of the
integrity of the Scriptures — witness, for example,
Lew Wallace, author of the historical novel *Ben Hur.*

We could fill this book with a list of great and
influential minds which have been convinced of the
Bible's claim to be God's Word. In most cases it was
their submission to the Word of God which ener-
gized and liberated them for the striking academic
and practical exploits in which they engaged. Our list
would include the names of scientists like Sir Isaac
Newton, Blaise Pascal, Michael Faraday and Sir
John Ambrose Fleming; men of letters like Augustine
of Hippo, William Cowper, James Montgomery and
Daniel Defoe; and such household names as Felix
Mendelssohn and Henry J. Heinz. And what shall we
say of the millions of ordinary men and women who
have come to know God in a personal way through
the message of the Bible? There is not time to
recount how whole nations and cultures have taken
a new direction simply because of the influence of a
single book of about 1000 pages. Our history books
are full of such incidents, and the evidence is there
for all to see.

The Bible is still under attack, and still triumph-
ing. Archaeologists, who only a few years ago dog-
matically declared that John's reference to a
pavement called 'Gabbatha' (John 19:13) was a mistake, now wonder how they ever missed it. It was

only fifteen feet under modern Jerusalem, and
measures fifty yards by fifty yards! They shelter
under the porticoes of Bethesda (John 5:2), which
they so recently said did not exist! They date the
whole of the New Testament round Luke's statement in Acts 18:12 that 'Gallio was proconsul of
Achaia', because they now know the exact dates
when he occupied that office — having said only a
few years before that the said Gallio, brother of
Seneca, never enjoyed that position! They retract
their bold assertion that John's Gospel was written
in the second century, because an extract from it
has been found in the wrappings of an Egyptian
mummy known to have died late in the first century! As knowledge advances, those who attack the
Bible have to eat humble pie more and more often.
Many of its critics are now completely conquered.

It is widely imagined today that modern scientific
discovery has disproved the Bible. This is a myth.
There are tens of thousands of scientists who believe
the Bible exactly as it stands. They come from all
branches of the sciences, and many of them are
acknowledged leaders in their particular fields. The
Bible is not at variance with any proven scientific
fact. Those who think that the theory of evolution
overthrows the Bible will certainly be interested
in the three books I have recommended at the end
of this chapter, two of which are written by scientists
of international repute. There is no fact known to
modern man which need shake our faith in the
integrity of the Scriptures. Prejudice and unbelief
are found among scientists as much as among any
other group of people. Their scientific training does
not make them infallible, and we need to test their
statements by the very scientific method which
they themselves espouse. When we do so, we find

that no established fact disproves the Scriptures. Indeed, the very opposite is true. Many modern discoveries have dramatically confirmed them.

There is no book like the Bible! From whatever angle we approach it, we are driven again and again to the conclusion that it can be nothing other than the Word of God.

> The Bible *is* we plainly see,
> Then it must have a pedigree.
> It either is a book divine,
> Or men to make it must combine;
> Suppose the latter, then they must
> Either be wicked men, or just.
> Take either side and you will see
> A proof of its divinity.
>
> If *wicked* men composed this book
> Surely their senses they forsook,
> For they the righteous man defend
> And curse the bad from end to end.
> If *righteous,* then they change their name,
> For they the authorship disclaim,
> And often say, 'Thus saith the Lord,'
> And testify it is His Word.
> If it be *not* they tell a lie,
> And all their righteousness destroy.
>
> *Could* Moses and *could* Malachi
> Unite together in a lie?
> *Could* Job and Daniel with the rest,
> Spread o'er the world from east to west,
> Unite together and confer,
> When oceans rolled between them, sir?
> Not only seas, but ages too,
> Numbers of years and not a few.

The teaching of Jesus

The second reason why Christians trust the Bible is
because of the teaching of Jesus Christ. Almost
2,000 years ago there came into the world a person
whom they believe to be none other than God
incarnate. The reasons for this conviction are given
in chapter 5, so there is no advantage in going over
them here. It is because Jesus set his seal on the
fact that the Bible is God's Word that Christians
believe it, too, for 'A disciple is not above his teacher,
nor a servant above his master' (Matthew 10:24).

The Scriptures which our Lord had in his hand
were identical to our present Old Testament. A Jewish sect called the Sadducees rejected most of these
Scriptures and only accepted the parts which they
thought were reasonable. For them, human reason
was the most important thing of all. Another sect
called the Pharisees accepted all the Old Testament
books, but laid even greater importance on the
writings and opinions of their forefathers and consistently submitted to the latter when they con-
flicted with the Scriptures. For them, religious
tradition occupied the place of supreme importance.

Not so our Lord. In all disputed points of belief
and behaviour, it was to the Scriptures that he
turned. He accepted them without reserve and
framed his whole life and teaching in the light of
them. He quoted them at the beginning and end of
his public ministry, and at every turn in between.
His life was one of continual and reverent study
of the sacred books, and his confidence in them
was complete.

Jesus clearly recognized that human authors
penned the words that he so frequently quoted.
Equally clearly he taught that *God* was the true
Author — not only of the ideas expressed, but of

the very words. This is why he used such expressions as 'David himself said by the Holy Spirit' (Mark 12:36, quoting from Psalm 110:1); and why, at one point, he made the whole force of his argument depend upon a single Old Testament word! (John 10:34.) For him the Scriptures were entirely factual, accurate and truthful. No mistake was possible in them, for 'the Scripture cannot be broken' (John 10:35). Their divine origin made them entirely authoritative, for 'Your word is truth' (John 17:17).

The Scriptures of our Lord's day were a known collection. It was the books of that collection, and no others whatever, that he accepted as the infallible Word of God. It is easy to see, then, why Christians do not accept as Scripture the books of the *Apocrypha*. But on what grounds do they accept the twenty-seven books of the New Testament, and put them on an equal footing with the thirty-nine books of the Old?

Our Lord gathered around him a small and diverse band of men whom he called 'apostles', who accompanied him throughout his public ministry. To them he committed the important task of both recording and explaining the facts and meaning of his life, death and resurrection. He promised them that they would enjoy the help and ministry of the Holy Spirit in doing so. The promised Spirit would bring to their mind all that they needed to remember and would protect them from error (John 14:26; 15:26; 16:13). In this way the early Christian church was built upon the ministry of the apostles, who became known as its 'foundation' (Ephesians 2:20). From the very first it was recognized that they were clothed with the authority of Christ himself — the Christ with whom they had been in such intimate contact.

All the New Testament books were written by
these apostles, or by those who laboured under their
superintendence — except for the Epistles of Paul,
and Luke and Acts, which were written under Paul's
superintendence. Paul was appointed an apostle by
the risen Lord himself, and his apostleship and
writings were endorsed by the original apostles
(Acts 26:15–20; Galatians 2:7–10; 2 Peter 3:15–
16). He therefore honourably takes his place among
the Master's special men, endued as much as they
with the authority of Christ himself. We accept the
books that his commissioned representatives have
written, as much as if they had been written by the
incarnate God himself.

Spiritual eyes and ears
This does not yet exhaust the reasons given for the
unwavering trust that Christians have in the Bible.
There is a third. It is to do with the fact that
Christians have more than five senses.

The Bible teaches that the person who has
repented and believed the gospel can see things
which other people cannot. Restored to him is a
spiritual faculty which others have lost. The spiritual
world is a reality to him, and he recognizes spiritual
things when he meets them. By means of this faculty
he clearly sees that the Bible is the book from God
which it claims to be: 'But the natural man does not
receive the things of the Spirit of God, for they are
foolishness to him; nor can he know them, because
they are spiritually discerned' (1 Corinthians 2:14).

Jesus put it another way. He described himself as
the Good Shepherd, and those who come to believe
in him as his sheep. He said of the Shepherd, 'The
sheep follow him, for they know his voice. And a
stranger they will by no means follow, but will flee

from him, for they do not know the voice of strangers . . . My sheep hear My voice, and I know them, and they follow Me' (John 10:4–5, 27).

Jesus' endorsement of the Old Testament and his commissioning of the apostles to write the New mean that the Bible is the place where his voice speaks. Those who are his 'sheep' hear his voice there, while others do not. At the end of the day a person's embrace of the Bible is the result of spiritual discernment. Those who have experienced a spiritual change of nature can no longer accept it as the word of men, but must welcome it for what it is in truth — the Word of God.

A person born blind can never be convinced that the sunset is beautiful, however powerful may be the logic of the argument. He may perhaps give lip-service to what he hears, but it means nothing to him personally until he *sees* the sunset for himself. For this to happen, his blindness must be cured. For some, the very sunshine which they cannot see has been the means of healing their eyes. In the same way, exposure to the Bible is the solitary means which God uses to dispel spiritual blindness and to effect the eye-opening spiritual change which it calls 'the new birth': 'Having been born again, not of corruptible seed but incorruptible, through the word of God which lives and abides forever' (1 Peter 1:23).

Those who are born again in this way have no trouble in believing the Bible's own claims concerning its character. Here are two of them, the first from the apostle Peter, and the second from the apostle Paul: 'No prophecy of Scripture is of any private interpretation; for prophecy never came by the will of man, but holy men of God spoke as they were moved by the Holy Spirit' (2 Peter 1:21). 'All Scripture is given by inspiration of God, and is profitable for doctrine, for reproof, for correction, for instruction in righteousness, that the man of God may be complete, thoroughly equipped for every good work' (2 Timothy 3:16—17).

It is only a short step from believing these claims to crying with the psalmist, 'O how I love Thy law! It is my meditation all the day' (Psalm 119:97).

To pursue this subject:

How we got our Bible and why we believe it is God's Word by W. H. Griffith Thomas. (Paperback, Moody Press.)
**Nothing but the Truth* by Brian H. Edwards. (Paperback, Evangelical Press.)
***The Voice of Authority* by George W. Marston. (Paperback, Presbyterian and Reformed Publishing Company.)

On the theory of evolution:

Bone of Contention by Sylvia Baker. (Magazine-format booklet, Evangelical Press.)
**From Nothing to Nature* by Professor E. H. Andrews. (Paperback, Evangelical Press.)
***The Natural Sciences know nothing of Evolution* by Dr A. E. Wilder-Smith. (Paperback, Creation-Life Publishers.)

3.
Is there any purpose in man's existence?

A Swiss girl was trying to learn English. On seeing someone do something rather surprising, she intended to ask, 'What on earth are you doing?' It came out rather differently, as she enquired, 'What are you doing on earth?'

It is this question which this chapter comes to examine. Why are we here? Why do we exist? I am living my life — but what is life *for*? I exist — but what is the *purpose* of my existence? I am alive — but for what *reason*? How am I to answer the question: 'What are you doing on earth?'

What modern man is saying
Through the centuries, people of all cultures have wrestled with this problem, and have tried to work out the answer for themselves. Modern thinkers are still trying to do the same.

One of the most influential thinkers of modern times has been the Frenchman, Jean-Paul Sartre (1905—1980), a novelist, dramatist and existential philosopher. His message to our times can be put like this: 'There is no God. Here you are in the world, whether you like it or not. You may as well make the best of it. But remember, whatever you do, you will soon be dead; so it really will have been a waste of time doing it. At the end of the day, life has no meaning. There is no reason for our being here.'

Equally influential has been the English philosopher and mathematician, Bertrand Russell (1872—

1970). His thinking can be put like this: 'There is no God. When you die, you will rot and that will be the end of it. There is nothing more. Meanwhile we live in a horrible world — a world full of tensions and made dark by the constant threat of nuclear devastation. This is where we spend our days. The aim of life is life itself, and it is too bad that death is the end. While we are here we ought to give ourselves to making the world a better place. We can do it if we try hard enough, and human life can reach heights that it has not yet attained. We do not need religion or superstition, for they only get in the way of this important task. Let us face the facts and get on with it.'

We probably think that the views of these philosophers have nothing to do with us. But such men write books, which teachers and educators read. Eventually their views percolate downwards, until they are aired by the media and embraced by the man in the street.

The proverbial man in the street already accepts that he owes his origins to evolution from lower forms of life. This view began as a scientific hypothesis debated by scientists. It then became taught as a theory, and is now widely believed by most ordinary people to be a fact. This is an excellent example of this principle of 'percolation'. Another is the theories of Higher Criticism which also began in the middle of the last century. It was an academic movement which began to cast doubts on the trustworthiness of the Bible. Although, like evolution, its views have never been demonstrated to be true, it is a fact that most people today believe that somehow the Bible has been shown to be unreliable.

There is plenty of evidence that ordinary men and women, besides absorbing evolution and Higher

Criticism, have already absorbed the views of Sartre and Russell. None of us would be surprised to hear the following paragraphs. We have heard something similar hundreds of times. It is the way that people all around us have come to think.

'I don't know if there is a God or not. We simply can't be sure. If there is one, I don't suppose he is interested in me.

'As for myself, I am the result of evolution. I just "happen" to be here, and there is no plan behind it that I can see. Where we go from here is anybody's guess. Perhaps there is an after-life, but again perhaps there isn't.

'The world is too depressing for words. It is filled with troubles, the threat of war, the breakdown of society and a thousand other things too distressing to mention. I would prefer to forget about them as much as I can, and to get on with enjoying myself. Life is short, and I want to make the most of it, getting through it as comfortably as possible.

'Of course I haven't forgotten that there are other people here in the world with me, and I want to help them all I can. But I don't see why they should get in the way of the things that I want to do.

'I suppose I would describe myself as a sort of pagan, who is doing his best to find happiness. I'm willing to work, but can't see why I should overdo it. Money seems to be the best thing to go for. It will buy me the things that will make my life more comfortable, and it will also get me the entertainments and pleasures that will help me to escape a little.'

The fact is that modern men and women simply *do not know* what is the purpose of their existence. They confess to believing that we *cannot* know.

Most, caught up in lives they have made for themselves, confess that they do not even *want* to know.
Such deep questions are a distraction from the quest
in hand.

Yet all the time the human conscience is not
entirely satisfied with this position. It is declared
that human life is meaningless, and that man is little
different from the animals. But, deep down inside
them, those who say such things are not so sure.
When pushed into a corner they will admit that man
is *not* the same as the animals. There is more to him
than that.

This reveals itself in a multitude of ways. For
example, every day in Britain thousands of cats are
sterilized. Yet when recently there was talk of
sterilizing a girl without her consent, there was a
public outcry.

Let us take another example. Whole species of
creatures have become extinct in recent years without
a word of publicity, but when thirty people are
killed in an overturned coach it is headline news.
Jacques Cousteau calculated that between 1965 and
1975, 50% of life in the world's oceans was killed
by pollution. This announcement caused no alarm
and has been all but forgotten. Yet when lesser-
known names declared that the human race could
die from the same cause within a few generations,
it was enough for whole governments to shape new
policies regarding their use of the environment.
Animals are one thing, but humans are another.
Even those who do not turn a hair at present-day
ravages of the animal kingdom consider that the
destruction of the human race 'ought not' to happen.
Why are men and women so special? Why does the
human conscience universally recognize that they
are?

Despite what academics are writing, despite what the man in the street says, each person knows in his heart of hearts that his life has a meaning which animal life does not have. He knows that he is not the same. There is *more* to man than that. Although he may not have given much thought to it, his conscience tells him that there is a reason for being here after all. There is a meaning to his existence. There is some higher and better purpose for mankind than for other creatures.

The Bible has the answer

What is that purpose, and where do we find out about it? We discovered in our first chapter that we need not doubt that God *is*, and that the God who *is* is the God of the Bible. Our second chapter demonstrated that we need have no qualms at all about unreservedly accepting what the Bible teaches.

In a world of confusion, frustration, unhappiness and restlessness, the Bible alone spells out a clear message for us. It tells us why we are here and what life is for. It unveils the reason and the purpose of human existence. It tells us what we should be doing on earth. What now follows is a summary of what the Word of God says on this point. We could easily give Bible references to support each statement, but these would so obviously interrupt the flow of the chapter that they have not been included. This book, after all, is only a starting-point.

The Bible tells me that I cannot possibly understand why I am here until I know exactly *what I am*. I am not the fruit of random chances — an evolutionary accident who just 'happens' to be here. I am not something which is here for no particular reason and without purpose. I am not an entity whose existence has no meaning.

The very opposite is true. I am a creature. It is by recognizing this fact that my search for purpose begins to come to a happy conclusion. I am a creature. Man is a direct creation of God who has been designed for specific reasons, and is here for a definite purpose. We have been made *by* another, *for* another. We have not been made for ourselves, but for him — and this is the fact which makes our existence full of meaning. As long as we leave God out of the picture, we will be confused about the purpose of our lives; but once we put him back, everything becomes as clear as day.

A parable

We can explain this truth in the most boring manner possible, or by the use of an illustrative story, or parable. I, for one, would prefer the latter method.

Some people who had built a splendid bungalow on the very edge of the jungle had to leave it in a hurry. Shortly after their departure their empty home was visited by a jungle-dweller. He had never seen anything like it before and wandered from room to room gaping with amazement.

Not everything in the house was new to him. There was a melon left in the fruit-bowl, which he quickly ate. On the verandah was some water in a bucket. The bucket was quite unlike the receptacles used in the jungle, but did not seem strange to the visitor. Very soon he was able to work out what the chairs and beds were used for, and switched the lights on and off without dismay. He was really very much at home.

But there were a number of objects which perplexed him entirely. What were *they* for? One of them was a round flat disc, made of a shiny black material which he had never seen before. On each side it had a long scratch which began at the edge, and ended shortly before the middle, where there was a hole.

Try as he might, he simply could not fathom what this disc was for. Many ideas went through his mind, but none of them fitted the bill. It could not be eaten. It was inefficient as a fan. It did not make a very interesting toy. Because all his guesses failed he eventually concluded that there was no particular reason why the disc was in the house. It served no obvious purpose. It was an object without meaning. With a grunt of disapproval, he threw it away!

He viewed the disc exactly as modern philosophers view man. He is here without a reason. This leads to the idea that he can easily be discarded. It is no accident that the rise of modern philosophy has gone hand in hand with the social acceptance of abortion, infanticide and euthanasia. Once it is believed that man's existence is meaningless, he is not regarded with the same value as before. In certain circumstances he can be dispensed with.

If the owners of the bungalow had returned to find the stranger in their lounge, they could have solved his problem immediately. They could have placed the disc on the turntable of the record-player, and as soon as he heard the music, he would have understood.

A disc, on its own, is meaningless, but put it *where it is meant to be* (if you like, in a 'right relationship' with the record-player), and the purpose of its creation is obvious. You now know why it exists, and what it is doing in the house. Records are meant to make music. That is what they are *for*. Link them up in a correct way with a record player, and they *do*. Until then they are a nonsense.

Men and women are meant for God, and their

existence has no meaning when separated from him.
God created the first man to know and to enjoy him.
He was made in God's image and was capable of
having fellowship with his Creator. He was designed
to find his highest satisfaction in having God as his
Friend. He was intended to live the whole of his life
in devoted dependence upon God, to obey him and
to find blissful pleasure in pleasing him by every task
that he performed. It was God's intention that his
highest creature should live for his glory, and should
enjoy him *for ever.*

Man was also to enjoy God's world and to manage
it on his behalf. He was to possess it all and to harness
its resources for his own welfare and good. He was to
cultivate its soil and also to be over all its other
creatures. The divine plan was that God's companions
should enjoy his world thoroughly.

While man walked with God, all went according to
plan. The record was on the machine and the music
was sweet. But now the music of that early harmony
has gone, although it lingers on a little in man's
constitution. He still has a 'spiritual' side to his
nature, despite the fact that God seems distant from
him. He cultivates the ground, is superior to the
animals and harnesses the world's resources — but all
with difficulty and toil, and an inescapable sense of
frustration. Golden moments of pleasure do not make
up for the lost bliss of Eden. The spectre of approach-
ing death haunts every human heart with fear. What
has gone wrong? How did the record leave the
machine, and thus cause the music to stop? How did
man and his Creator become so tragically separated?

What has gone wrong
Perhaps a continuation of our parable will help us to
see how incredibly foolish our race has been. The

music has stopped because the record has left the machine, and has become spoiled in the process. The fault was not with the machine. That is as perfect as ever. The record simply thought that it could play better music *itself*! It persuaded itself that it no longer needed the machine, and that a better future awaited it if it struck out on its own. It was talked into this course of action by a lying serpent, but the fault is its own. It has never made music since. It retains many of its original characteristics, but lies distorted on the floor.

On the floor the record persuades itself that all is well. Yet it can never escape the inner conviction that it was made for something better and higher, and that it is capable of serving a purpose much more exalted than its present meaningless existence.

If that conviction were not there, it could tolerate its present position much more comfortably. It is not without significance that both Sartre and Russell had to preface their statements about meaninglessness with the remark that there is no God. If there is no such thing as a record-player, nor ever has been, *of course* records are objects without meaning. But every human conscience knows differently. Statements of atheism are nothing more than negative responses to what every human heart knows to be true. God *is*, and we were made for him. The record's sense of purpose and search for meaning are doomed to remain frustrated as long as it stays on the floor. Nothing less than a return to the turntable will do. But to admit that would also mean admitting that we have been wrong all this time. This is something which the human heart is notoriously reluctant to do.

Every now and again the record on the floor has reminders that it was made for something better. All around it are tacks and pins, called money, excitement, friendship, entertainment, prestige, etc. When these things come into contact with the record's grooves, it gives off a short sound. For a moment it appears that it has found an alternative way of making its original music. But it is an illusion. The sound soon dies away, and certainly bears little resemblance to the continual hi-fi quality which the record knew generations ago. What looked so promising always proves to be a disappointment. Not only so, but each such encounter leaves the disc scratched, and more spoiled than before.

The music of life can never be heard except on a record restored to the turntable. All mankind's troubles spring from its separation from God. The greatest need of each individual is reconciliation to him. Being near the record-player will not do. The record needs to be *on* it again!

Getting right
The gospel announces that God lifts up spoiled records — even those which are worse than all the rest — and that he places them on the turntable again! The hands which lift are those of Jesus Christ, which were wounded in the process. The reason for this is explained in chapter 6. He came right onto the floor, where his announcement was 'I have come that they may have life, and that they may have it more abundantly' (John 10:10). Each record that he lifts up, he relabels, and it is his for ever. He also removes some of their blemishes right away, and others as the months and years go by. They make music again! The time is coming when he will melt and remould them all perfectly, and then the music they play will be vastly superior to even that which sounded from Adam at the beginning of the world. It will be an endless symphony of unspoiled happiness and perfect praise.

Almost without exception, the records which remain on the floor tend to resent those who have returned to God. The music which they hear strikes them as surpassingly strange. It is so unlike anything that they have been able to make themselves that they consider it to be odd, and even bizarre. It provokes all sorts of reactions, including laughter, jealousy and bitterness. It makes many resolve to remain exactly as they are, and never to change. Others greet the new music with opposition and cruelty. But although the taunts of others can be deeply hurtful, none of these things can ever destroy the happiness and fulfilment of those who have been restored to fellowship with their Maker. They have begun to love, serve and enjoy God, and at last to understand what this life is *for*. The whole of their lives is coloured with this perspective, and they have increasing anticipation of the further glories which await them. Their quest for some meaning to life has ended, although their enjoyment of life has truly only just begun.

They have found what they were looking for, and the conscience of every other person knows that they have, too. For those who are still far from God, they have a message. It is 'We implore you in Christ's behalf, be reconciled to God' (2 Corinthians 5:20).

There are those who heed the message and cry, in their turn, 'God be merciful to me a sinner!' (Luke 18:13.) God comes at once to such suppliants, who therefore immediately enter into the enjoyment of fellowship with him. 'For everyone who exalts himself will be abased, and he who humbles himself will be exalted' (Luke 18:14). They never again ask the question which is the title of this chapter.

To pursue this subject:

*Men of Destiny by Peter M. Masters. (Paperback, Wakeman.)

**The God of the Bible by Robert P. Lightner. (Paperback, Baker Book House.)

***Understanding the Times by G. I. Williamson. (Paperback, Presbyterian and Reformed Publishing Company.)

4.
What has gone wrong with the world?

Everybody believes that something is wrong with the world.

One day in Hyde Park, London, I saw a very ordinary man addressing an immense crowd. He announced that he was going to make three statements, and challenged anybody present to contradict any one of them. His first statement was 'There is something wrong with the world today.' Not a person murmured.

Everybody believes that something is wrong with the world. It is a daily subject of conversation wherever men and women meet together. The discussion ranges over a wide variety of topics, but the conclusion is always the same. Wars and revolutions on the international scene; strikes and disputes at home; vandalism, crime and the problems of young people; the rise of violence in our streets; riots in inner-city areas; the spirit of discontent and the disappearance of the old neighbourliness of years ago — all these things are appealed to in support of the contention that the world is not what it should be.

Has it ever been any different?
The interesting thing is that the world does not appear ever to have been any different. What are your memories of history lessons at school? Lesson after lesson seemed to be little more than a catalogue of war, hate, intrigue and violence. There is no crime committed today of which we cannot read in any

century of our choosing. Industrial strikes are an
emotive subject, but they were known in ancient
Rome — even among slaves! Graffiti horribly defaces
many of our modern buildings, but the excavation
of Pompeii showed that that city had the same
problem, and its slogans were far worse than anything we see ourselves. No ancient civilization was
free from the ravages of vandalism. All the evidence
is that mankind has always been discontented,
greedy, selfish and spiteful.

The world has never been any different. Why,
then, should we think that there is anything wrong
with it? Concerning our present ills, we would
expect men and women to say, 'Such behaviour is
only *natural*. Things have always been this way.'
But they do not. The response in this and previous
generations has been that these things *ought not* to
be so. In every person's mind there is a gap between
what the world *is* and what it *should* be. Things have
never been any different, and yet the human conscience considers that it is *wrong* for things to be the
way they are.

Wherever mankind has been found, and in whatever century, his life has been filled with strife. His
history is that of nation against nation, communities
at loggerheads with each other, tensions between
neighbours, misunderstandings at work, arguments
within the family, and even a person at variance with
himself. The spirit of alienation runs through the
race. Nobody is free from it, and yet everybody
thinks that it ought not to be so.

There are few, if any people, who have never
stolen. Yet stealing is condemned everywhere. Hate-
ful thoughts are a universal experience, but when
they lead to their logical conclusion of revenge or
murder, all societies are horrified. Adultery is

considered to be all right if it is done voluntarily, or happens 'somewhere else', but when our own partner is involved the situation is considered to be intolerable. All people lie at times, but resent being lied to. We are willing to set our heart on the property of others, but feel offended when we see somebody casting their eyes over our own.

The world has always been like this. In people's hearts there seems to be written a set of principles which they consider to be right, although they do not live by them themselves! Man has never lived by these principles, and yet he feels that he *ought* to have done. It is this gap between what the world has always been, and what each person thinks it *should* be like, which gives rise to the conviction that something has gone wrong with the world. It is as if there is a sort of 'memory', which has been passed on from parent to child, saying that although history suggests that things have always been like this, there was none the less a time when they were *not*. We cannot rid ourselves of the feeling that our race is not what it should be. It is a feeling that haunts us throughout our lives, and never leaves us alone. We excuse ourselves by saying, 'Nobody's perfect,' but then condemn the same fault in others! All our hearts know that there is a standard from which the human race has slipped. We have never seen anybody live up to that standard, but the *idea* of it is engraved into our consciences, and we cannot shake it off.

Observation gives us a clear picture of what our race is like — a picture which tallies exactly with the Bible's description. No other book in the world tells us the truth about ourselves. Only the Bible has got it right. Its description is spot on!

We saw in chapter 2 that this fact is one of the

reasons that we can have unreserved confidence in
the Scriptures. They tell us the truth in the areas
that we can check up for ourselves, so there can be
no reason to distrust them in those areas which we
cannot observe.

Man has a sense of absolute law in his heart — the
Bible tells us so; but we can also see it for ourselves.
He does not live by this law, although he expects
others to do so. His conscience troubles him, but
still does not restrain him from selfish actions. He
knows that things are not what they used to be,
and not what they should be, but he does not know
how to be any different. All these things the Bible
tells us, and all these things we also know from our
own observation.

So far so good. What the Bible teaches us, and
what we see, exactly agree. But there are a vast
number of questions which we cannot answer ourselves, because the answers cannot be found in the
realm of observation. For instance, how did the
sense of 'law' get into the human heart in the first
place? Why, precisely, are we so slow to blame ourselves, and much quicker to blame others? What was
the original world like, of which we have some sort
of inherited memory? How did the human race slip
from the standard which is still engraved on its
conscience, and get into its present state? What is
the hope of its ever being any different?

All these questions are answered in the Bible.
Having seen its integrity in every area where we
can verify it, shall we not now trust it in these other
areas, too? At the very least, we ought to listen to
it seriously. What are the biblical answers to our
unanswered questions?

What does the Bible say?

The Bible's teaching can be summarized simply. The whole of creation has gone wrong, because God's last and finest creation has gone wrong. Man is the keystone of creation — the very apex. The keystone has been broken, and the whole arch has collapsed. No stone is in its right place any more. The whole structure is out of joint. The fall of man is the cause of the whole of the disorientation of this universe.

Have you ever read the first three chapters of the Bible — Genesis 1—3? It is here that both the creation and the Fall of man are recorded. No one who is interested in what has gone wrong with the world can afford to ignore these pages, because here is the very foundation for all else that the Bible teaches on this subject.

These chapters tell us that the creation of man and woman was God's final act of creation, and was different from all that went before. God is a plurality as well as a unity, and before this event he took solemn counsel with himself. The creation of man himself was an immediate act. He was made from the ground, and shortly afterwards woman was made from him. It is interesting that modern genetics confirm that the whole of woman (XX) was made from half of man (XY). Unlike all the other creatures, mankind was made after a divine type, or 'in the image of God', as the Bible puts it. From the very beginning there was a physical side to his make-up, and also an invisible side, which was breathed into him directly by God. It is the divine bringing together of these two elements which makes man *man*. He is not just a physical machine. There is more to him than that. It was this unique creation which was the highest creature which God made, and to whom he gave dominion over the whole of the rest of creation.

Many people are perplexed by the teaching that man was made 'in the image of God'. What does it mean? We can put it like this. God has being, and so does man. But there is a difference. God's being is eternal and underived, while man receives his power *to be* from God. God is wise, and man is the wisest thing on earth. God is powerful, and nothing on earth is more powerful than man. God is holy, and so was man originally — and he still has an obvious moral sense, as we have seen. God is good, man was also perfectly good at the beginning, and is far from entirely devoid of goodness today. God is just, and man, alone of all creatures, has a sense of justice — seen in noble ways, such as in his institutions to promote justice, and also seen in depraved ways, such as in his frequent desires for revenge. It is also seen in the oft-repeated complaint: 'It's not fair!' God is truth, and man in his heart still praises the truth and despises all departures from it.

There is an obvious likeness between man and God, even today. All these attributes are clearly spoiled in mankind, but they are still *there* none the less. However, even if they were perfect, there would still be vast differences between these attributes in God and the same attributes in us. In God each one of them is infinite, eternal and unchangeable. In man each one is limited, temporal and prone to change. But this does not alter the fact that man is unique in these points, as well as in other characteristics, such as the power to love, to appreciate the abstract, to communicate in language and to be creative and inventive. Man is not in any physical likeness to God. How could he be? God, by definition, is a Spirit, and without a body. But the likeness between man and God is none the less obvious, and he is unique in having this likeness. It is this feature about man which is described by the biblical teaching that he was made 'in the image of God'.

Man's 'God-thirst' or religious sense is a left-over from something much better which he had before his Fall. At that time he was morally perfect and enjoyed unhindered communion with God. Adam knew God and 'walked' with him. It was a relationship of perfect fulfilment and unspoiled happiness. If the Fall had not taken place, Adam and Eve would have walked with God for ever, and would never have died. Death is an invasion from outside. It is not natural, and it was never God's desire that we should experience it. This explains why we fear it. It is God's punishment for the sin of our race. If sin had never entered this world, nor would death have done so.

God's covenant with Adam
This point leads us to mention that God entered into a covenant with Adam. He gave Adam marvellous privileges, but also made certain demands upon him. His privileges were not restricted to the uniqueness of his constitution. God placed him in circumstances which were nothing less than paradise. There he gave to him the gift of work and the enjoyment of eating the fruits of the garden of Eden. The labour was sweet and contained no element of frustration or toil, as it has done since the Fall. Every aspect of the creation was subordinate to him, and nothing in it endangered him. Marriage was given to him as a holy institution and, despite the Fall, no culture has yet been able to eradicate from its conscience the idea that marriage is 'right' and that uncovenanted relationships between men and women lack an important element.

The pleasures of Adam's work did not mean he had to be at it all the time. His life was patterned on God's creation of the world, and in memory of it. He worked six days, but every seventh day was a day of complete rest, or a 'sabbath' (Hebrew: 'rest'). It is worth underlining the fact that it was not the Ten Commandments which established the sabbath day, but that its origin goes back to the beginning of the world. The whole concept of the *week* is written deep into the fabric of human life. We get our year from the time it takes the earth to go round the sun. Our month is roughly based on the circuits of the moon around the earth. But where does the week come from? It is wherever mankind is found, and all attempts to alter the weekly cycle to a greater or lesser number than seven days have resulted in abysmal failure — witness the attempts after the French Revolution or among the early Bolsheviks. Adam was made for God, and walked in living communion with him all the time. But once a week he stopped everything else he was doing, and spent a whole day doing *nothing else* except enjoying the company of his Creator. It is from such a pleasurable association with the Invisible that our race has fallen.

So much for Adam's privileges, but what were the things which God demanded from him in that early covenant? He and his wife were expected to be obedient to God. They knew what his will was, because his law was written into their consciences, and they also walked with him without interruption. Their obedience was expected to be perfect, and also perpetual. As a pledge that such obedience was the way to enjoy the continued and endless favour of God, there was found in their garden 'the tree of life'. But there was also another tree, which they were forbidden even to touch, on pain of death. This was 'the tree of the knowledge of good and evil' (Genesis 2:9). People often ask why there had to be such a tree, but if we think it through it should become clear to us. Adam was not a puppet. He was a moral creature made in God's image, who was expected to be perfectly obedient to him. Where there is no alternative to obedience, can there be *real* obedience? If it is to convince anyone that it is genuine, it needs to be tested.

The Fall and its effects

Adam failed the test and broke the covenant. It began when the tempter sowed seeds of doubt, unbelief and pride in Eve's mind. Very soon Adam was implicated. Neither of them continued to take God's threats seriously. What he had forbidden seemed harmless and even desirable. In a spirit of inexcusable rebellion they disobeyed his clear command and the covenant lay in pieces. It was the worst act of wickedness the world has ever known. God's instructions could not have been clearer. Both pledge and warning showed which path was safe to tread, and which was to be avoided. Adam and Eve were perfectly capable of saying, 'No,' to all evil suggestions, and of continuing to enjoy their Creator's smile. But they walked out on it all and preferred the evil to the good.

Who can ever adequately convey the effects of that sin upon Adam and Eve themselves? Their holy natures now became twisted and polluted with sinful thoughts and affections. Their communion with God was lost and he has seemed 'far away' to every member of the human race ever since. A sense of moral defilement invaded their consciences, and they became guilty and ashamed. A new emotion thus entered the stream of human existence. Even at this stage God demonstrated his mercy and promised to the human race a suffering Saviour, but also made it clear that no sinner would ever find his *own* way back into the paradise from which humanity's first parents were expelled.

The whole of nature was to remind Adam and Eve and all their race of their extreme folly. For women the whole childbearing process was now to be one of pain. Man would find his work weighed down with toil and frustration. The fear of death would stalk through the whole race, and the grave would be the common destination of all.

This is the way sin entered the world. Sin is lawlessness. Adam and Eve flagrantly disobeyed God's clearly revealed will. The law written on their hearts is written on our hearts, too. It was underlined and renewed at Sinai, and was finally perfectly lived out among us by Jesus Christ. But it is disobeyed as much as ever.

Sin is contempt for God. If their hearts had reverenced him as they should, Adam and Eve would never have succumbed to the tempter's suggestions. But they came to regard God's rule as an unfair imposition. Men and women still do the same. They prefer God to keep out of their lives, provided that he will be near during moments of need. To live under his rule is an unthinkable suggestion. Life is much better if it is lived as if there were *no* God.

Sin is wickedness of heart. From Eden until now the human race has been characterized by hate, impurity, theft, lies, wanton desire and all the other features mentioned earlier in this chapter. Guilt has become a universal human experience. Our hearts know well enough that certain things 'ought not' to be done. We do them all the same, and then wake up in the night with moments of shame.

It is as plain as plain can be that Adam's sin has had permanent effects on the whole human race. He did not just ruin himself but us as well. Our representative failed, and we failed in him. We are also descended from him, and his fallen nature is as surely passed on to us as any other features inherited by children from their parents. We are sinners, too, not just by bias or imitation, but by nature. Each pair of human parents from Eden to the present has conceived nothing other than sinners like themselves.

It is as sinners that we come into the world, opposed to all spiritual good, and inclined to evil. It is because we are like this that we do actual *acts* of sin. By nature we are out of touch with God, whose holy anger we provoke with every lawless thought, word or deed. We cannot break the grip of evil upon us. He speaks to us through his creation, and through the Scriptures, but we do not hear his voice. By nature we are opposed to him and, despite the prickings of our conscience, are unwilling to change. We find it easier to believe what contradicts his Word, rather than his Word itself. We are more immediately attracted to the unlovely than to the holy.

The trouble which came into the world through our first parents has not lessened with the passing of the years. It strikes our nations, our own families and even our hearts. Some of it is physical, much of it is mental and most of it is spiritual. Each trouble brings its own pain. All the time our consciences remind us that things need never have been this way. Our high moments of pleasure, which God's continuing kindness still allows us, give us relief, but also serve as an eloquent reminder that without sin life would be nothing but perfectly happy.

Meanwhile we hasten to the grave, which for a person without God always comes too soon.

Our consciences horrify us by constantly assuring us that death is not the end. We know in our heart of hearts that we will give an answer to another for the way we have lived. There is to be a judgement, and the uncomfortable conviction of its certainty does not go away. What our consciences faintly know, God's Word tells us even more clearly. The separation of body and spirit which occurs at death is not the end of us. At last there will be a resurrection and every one of us shall give an account of himself to God. Unless our sins can be forgiven, and we can somehow be made righteous in the sight of God, we must surely endure the everlasting torment of body and soul in hell, which sin against an infinite God deserves. The thought of death fills us with fear. But the certainty of what lies beyond is terrifying.

An awful problem and its answer
Nothing appals us more than to hear of our lostness. If only we could reform our characters and be different! All of us have been able to make minor adjustments in our behaviour, but none of us has been able to change the sort of person we are. It is not new behaviour we need, but a new heart — not reformation, but regeneration. We can clearly see what has gone wrong with the world. It is *us*. 'For best results follow manufacturer's instructions,' we have often read. But we have not, and everything has gone haywire, and it is beyond us to put it right. Even if we could live perfectly from this moment, how could we ever make up for the months and years of wilful sin which have been such an offence to God, and which are still lodged in his memory? Even if we could now live perfectly, how could we stand before him when he demands an account of the *past*?

What has gone wrong with the world? This universe is like an old wheel, with a rim, spokes and hub. As long as the hub is in place the rim is sound, and the spokes are in a right relationship with each other. We have been foolish enough to try and do without the hub. The spokes have fallen apart, and person-to-person relationships are one of our greatest difficulties. Everything else has gone wrong, too. The whole organism is out of joint. Our consciences and God's Word both diagnose the real trouble. We no longer wonder what has gone wrong. Other great questions arise instead. How are things to be right? How am *I* to be put right, for surely that is the place to start. What is the way back to God?

The answer to this question is given to us in the gospel. It declares that men and women may, in *this* life, walk again with God. They may have all their sins forgiven and be put right in his sight. They may have him as their Father and know themselves to be his children. They may know his presence in their lives, be assured of his love and enjoy the peace of a good conscience. They may even have their characters changed by his power, and have a family feeling of unreserved acceptance with those everywhere who have entered into the same blessings. They may face the grave without terror, and with the strengthening comfort of being sure that he will never leave them nor forsake them — at the moment of death, or ever afterwards. They may live in the certainty of an untroubled resurrection, acquittal at the judgement, and an eternity experiencing joys greater than all those which were lost in Eden. All these things may be theirs without their ever deserving them, because of the Saviour whom God has appointed — the Lord Jesus Christ.

All these bold promises God makes to men and

women who live in this present fallen world. It was into this world that Jesus Christ came. It was in this arena of sin and temptation that he lived perfectly. Where all others have failed, he did not. It was his death and resurrection which secured the blessings that are promised to lost people in the gospel.

Who this Jesus Christ is, and why his cross was necessary, is explained in the next two chapters. The chapters after that explain how we may enter into the benefit of what he did for sinners, and also cast further light on what some of those benefits are.

To pursue this subject:

*Introducing the Christian Faith by John Keith Davies. (Booklet, Grace Publications Trust.)

**Right with God by John Blanchard. (Paperback, The Banner of Truth Trust.)

***The Christian Faith in the Modern World by J. Gresham Machen. (Paperback, William B. Eerdmans Publishing Company.)

5.
Who is Jesus Christ?

We have already mentioned the Lord Jesus Christ several times in this book. We now come to ask the crucial question. Was the carpenter of Nazareth really what he said he was — the Son of God? It is a question which has been asked in every century since he came among us, and reasonable people ask it still. Everything hinges on the answer. If his claims were not true, then we must write him off as a sheer impostor and liar, or as mentally deranged. However, if he *was* the Son of God, then the whole of the Christian gospel is established as true — for he is the source from which all of it flows.

Let us look at the picture of the Lord Jesus Christ which is given to us by the four Gospels, Matthew, Mark, Luke and John. Matthew and John were eye-witnesses of the earthly ministry of Christ. Luke, although not an eyewitness himself, compiled his Gospel from the testimony of such eyewitnesses, many of whom he interviewed personally — including Mary, Jesus' mother. Mark wrote his Gospel under the superintendence of Peter who, like John, was especially close to Christ during his earthly life. All four of these Gospels circulated widely during the lifetime of thousands of those who met Jesus for themselves, both friends and enemies alike. If they had contained any factual errors, there were plenty of people alive both to contradict and correct what was written. Nothing of the sort happened. The integrity of the Gospel records was accepted from the very beginning.

We can rely on what the Gospels tell us about Christ. In this chapter we shall simply summarize what they record on three themes — the claims, the character and the resurrection of Christ. These three themes are like the three lines which one must make to draw an arrow. On their own they mean very little, but put together they point us with certainty in the right direction. There is no mistaking what the Gospels expect us to believe about the identity of Christ. But we cannot be convinced against our will. The evidence points us to a clear conclusion, but it is a step of faith to accept Christ for what the Gospels portray him to be and to bow before him in a pledge of personal allegiance.

His claims

We start by mentioning the claims of Christ. As we search the Gospels we see that Jesus spoke a very great deal about himself. In this he was different from all the other great religious teachers of history. We can summarize their message as 'That is the truth, follow *that*,' whereas Jesus said, 'I am the truth, follow *Me*.' He claimed to be the bread which alone can give life, the light which alone can dispel the world's darkness and the only door to salvation. These claims were startling, and all the more so because each one began, 'I am . . .' 'I am' was recognized by the Jews as a claim to be God! Jesus Christ stood before the world and declared, 'I am the way, the truth, and the life. No one comes to the Father except through Me' (John 14:6).

Jesus claimed to be the Messiah promised for centuries by the Old Testament. He asserted that Abraham (2000 B.C.) saw him, that Moses (1500 B.C.) wrote of him and that every part of the Old Testament Scriptures was about him! He declared that man's chief duty was to believe on him, and that not to do so was his greatest sin. If anybody loved anything or anybody more than he loved Christ, he was not worthy of him. Not even a person's family may come first. And so it was to *himself* that he invited those who heard him: 'Come to me, all you who labour and are heavy laden, and I will give you rest. Take my yoke upon you and learn from Me, for I am gentle and lowly in heart, and you will find rest for your souls. For My yoke is easy and My burden is light' (Matthew 11:28–30).

Surely no one can read Christ's claims without astonishment. He is the King in God's kingdom. He is 'the Son of Man' — a title for the Messiah derived from the Old Testament. When Peter called him 'the Christ, the Son of the living God', he was commended for his insight. When the high priest put him on oath, and then asked him if he were the Son of God, his reply was 'It is as you said.' Such claims to deity are found scattered throughout the Gospels. His claim that God was uniquely his Father was well understood by the Jews, who accordingly took up stones to stone him. No less explicit was his statement: 'Most assuredly, I say to you, before Abraham was, I AM' (John 8:58). Nor did he turn away the confession of the worshipping Thomas, who addressed the risen Christ as 'My Lord and my God!' (John 20:28.)

Other claims of Christ were less direct, but equally obvious. Several times during his earthly ministry he claimed authority to forgive sins — a prerogative which belongs to God alone. Such claims were not made in a corner, and were in fact a major factor in bringing about the deterioration of relationships between him and the Jewish religious authorities. They were scandalized by such claims.

He claimed that he could give life — another divine

prerogative. He described himself, in turn, as the giver
of 'living water . . . springing up into everlasting life',
'the bread of life' and 'the resurrection and the life'.
He claimed to give such life to whomever he wanted,
and did not refuse Peter's assertion that he had 'the
words of eternal life'.

He claimed to teach the truth. The educated
scribes of the day conducted their discourses by
appealing to the opinions and writings of famous
scholars. Jesus spoke on his own authority, and
frequently began his sayings with the formula: 'Most
assuredly, I say to you . . .' Knowing full well that
he had nothing more than a village education, his
contemporaries could not understand from where
he acquired his wisdom, and often discussed it with
amazement. Jesus claimed that it came from God,
and that the words he spoke were the very words of
God (John 3:34). It was this conviction that lay
beneath everything he said. It led him to declare
that his words were eternal, and would remain even
when heaven and earth had passed away. His promises
were unfailing and his moral commands absolute. To
reject what he said was to reject the one who had
sent him.

He claimed that he would judge the world. All the
graves would give up their dead at the sound of his
voice. He would separate the whole human race into
two groups, just as Palestinian shepherds divided their
flocks of sheep and goats. Those to be welcomed into
glory would be welcomed by Christ himself. His
'I never knew you' would be the words consigning
all others to everlasting punishment. None who
believed on him in this life would be forgotten at the
last day, and his acknowledgement of them before
his Father would be enough to guarantee their
eternal safety.

What stupendous claims! Imagine someone *you* know making them! But added to these verbal claims were the claims implicit in his miracles. Christ performed many supernatural acts of power. These were not done to show off, but to convey certain lessons. They have been called 'acted parables'. For instance, his turning of water into wine at the wedding at Cana was an obvious claim to be inaugurating a new era. The feeding of the five thousand brought home something of his claim to be 'the bread of life'. His giving of sight to the man born blind went hand in hand with his claim to be 'the light of the world'. His claim to be 'the resurrection and the life' was stunningly underlined by his raising of Lazarus from the grave.

Such are Christ's claims — and there are many more, widely and evenly distributed throughout the four Gospels. The portrait is too consistent and too balanced to have been imagined. The claims are *there*! They really were made, and we must now decide what we are going to do with them. Were they deliberate lies? Are they the helpless statements of a man whose mind has gone? Could they be true? A look at Christ's character will help us to decide.

His character

Does the character of Jesus Christ bear out his claims, or does he have the well-known features of an impostor, or of someone who is insane?

The person portrayed in those early records does not bear the faintest resemblance to a deceiver or lunatic. He has a character entirely consistent with the claims we have mentioned. It is a character more wonderful than his greatest miracle. He is totally unlike any other person who has ever lived. Jesus Christ is in a moral category by himself. He is not the greatest of many names on a list. He is the Only.

He stands apart from us all. A holy and sinless life has been lived on this planet.

Jesus had the uncomfortable skill of being able to see right into the deepest recesses of people's hearts. When asked a question, he was able both to see and to reveal the motive of the questioner. Those who had hidden perplexities were not able to keep them a secret when Jesus was there. He could detect the slightest hypocrisy. It is acutely interesting that he who had such keen moral judgement showed not the slightest indication that there was any failure in his own life!

This fact alone makes Jesus unique. This earth has been graced by many men and women whose pure and honest lives have been widely admired. Without exception these same people have been deeply aware of their own shortcomings. This is plain from their diaries and personal papers and their conversations with intimate friends. Such outstanding people have always had a greater consciousness of their own failures than have more ordinary mortals.

But not so Jesus. He never confessed to any sin, never asked for forgiveness and never showed any sign that he had any awareness of personal guilt. His life contains no record of any moral failure and no trace that he himself was conscious of any. In a totally unassuming manner his words and actions reveal that he saw himself as without sin.

This is why Jesus remained alone to speak with the adulterous woman after her accusers had left her. He had asked any of them without sin to cast the first stone at her. Each of them left, one by one, but Jesus did not feel obliged to join them. He knew nothing of the sense of inward guilt which they so evidently felt. He alone was in a position to accuse the woman justly, but chose instead to forgive her and to encourage her to break with sin.

It was this inward sense of unpolluted purity which meant that Jesus could confidently ask his enemies, 'Which of you convicts Me of sin?' It also explains his earlier statement: 'The Father has not left Me alone, for I always do those things that please Him.' To Jesus, all other people were sheep, but he was the Shepherd. They were in the dark; he was the Light. They needed healing; he was the physician. All others were sinners; he was the Saviour. They were hungry, thirsty and dead. He was the bread, the living water and the life that they needed. Indeed, he was a man amongst men. But he was not *like* other people.

This was something the disciples clearly recognized. For over three years they lived and travelled with him and consequently knew him intimately. Others saw Jesus only in his public moments, but they observed him all the time. They saw him tired, hungry, thirsty and sad, and even witnessed him 'exceedingly sorrowful, even to death'. But they never saw in him the sins they found in themselves. Their familiarity with him did not breed contempt, but rather the increasing conviction that they were in company with a man without any sin or fault of any kind. This was a radical conclusion to reach. These men were Jews. They were soaked in the teachings of the Old Testament. To believe that a man could be perfect was against everything they had ever been taught. But this is precisely what they came to believe. Their testimony on the subject is especially arresting because they always mention their impressions as an 'aside' when talking about something else. They can never be accused of having an axe to grind and of labouring this point. But it was their certain conviction, and written into the very fabric of their thinking.

So it was that Peter described Jesus as 'a lamb without blemish and without spot . . . Who committed no sin, nor was guile found in His mouth' (1 Peter 1:19, 2:22). John calmly declared, 'In Him there is no sin' (1 John 3:5). This was the belief of all the early Christians. No living eye-witness ever managed to persuade them differently. We do not know of any who even tried. Jesus was referred to as him 'who knew no sin' (2 Corinthians 5:21) and as the one who was 'holy, harmless, undefiled, separate from sinners' (Hebrews 7:26).

This point was even conceded by Christ's enemies. They threw plenty of abuse at him during his earthly ministry! Their accusations included blasphemy, evil associations, frivolity and sabbath-breaking. But when at last it came to his trial, the only charges that they dared to bring were political, not moral. They had to employ false witnesses in order to secure a conviction. Even these could not agree among themselves! The whole affair was a gross mockery of justice. On the day of Christ's death Pontius Pilate, his wife, Herod, Judas Iscariot, the dying thief and the officiating centurion — all at different times proclaimed his innocency. There was, frankly, no fault in him.

Such a character was entirely consonant with Jesus' stupendous claim to be God manifest in the flesh. There was no trace of the crank in him. Unpopular he may have been, but he was not eccentric. He had all the physical limitations of human existence, but his character was that of God himself. There was a glorious consistency about him. He was always the same, in the obscurity of his peasant years or the public attention of preaching and

opposition. We see in Jesus a life free from all self-
interest. His was a life of perfect self-mastery — never
resentful, irritable or retaliating. Even when enduring
the shame and pain of being nailed to his cross, he
prayed that his Father would forgive his murderers!
There has never been anyone like him, or even near
him. He has been justly described as the 'man beyond
our reach'. We look on Jesus of Nazareth and see
God!

His resurrection

Two lines of our arrow have now been drawn, and we
therefore come to the central one which will make it
complete. The historical documents which record
his claims and tell of the character congruous with
them assert that on the Sunday after his crucifixion
he rose again from the dead! This line, like the others,
proves nothing on its own. But the three together
point very clearly to the deity of Christ. Only the
eyes of faith recognize his true identity, but it is
important to realize that such faith rests on an un-
erringly solid basis.

Have you ever considered the evidence for the
resurrection of Jesus Christ? History is full of men
and women who, on examining this evidence, have
come to believe in the resurrection as a historical
event. Very many of these began their examination
as cynics, sceptics or outspoken unbelievers. They
concluded that intellectual honesty could only be
maintained by accepting Christ's resurrection as a
fact.

Everyone who came to Jesus' tomb on the Sunday after his crucifixion found it to be empty! Many
of them came independently of each other, while
others ran to check the story that Jesus' body had
gone. Of course, it is entirely possible that some of

them went to the wrong tomb. But what about the
rest? Was everyone who visited the sepulchre that
day mistaken? There were those who had watched
the burial, and so knew exactly where to go. It is
true that some came in the dimness of early dawn,
but the vast majority came well after full light.
The tomb was clearly empty, and some explanation
must be given of it.

Through the years those who are not inclined to
believe in the resurrection have made all sorts of
suggestions as to why the tomb was empty. Nobody
doubts the fact. The disagreement has been about
how it came to be that way.

It has been suggested that Jesus was not actually
dead when he was buried. On the cross he fainted
and therefore appeared to be dead. The coolness
of the sepulchre revived him, and shortly afterwards
he rolled back the stone across the entrance and
persuaded his disciples that he was alive from the
dead!

Those who can believe this theory must be able
to believe almost anything. The Roman authorities
were sufficiently convinced that Jesus was dead
to have not hastened it by breaking his legs. To be
absolutely sure, a sword was thrust into his side.
Are we to believe that this bleeding and broken
form was then taken into a cold tomb, where he
remained for thirty-six hours with untended wounds,
and without food and drink — and survived? Are we
to understand that he then unfurled himself from his
winding grave-clothes (into which were wound about
a hundred pounds of spices), rolled back an immense
stone, escaped a Roman guard and managed to convince his disciples that he had conquered death,
before he crept away and died somewhere else
unnoticed?

Others suggest that thieves stole the body. But what was their motive? Why steal the emaciated corpse, and leave behind the only items of value — namely, the grave-clothes and spices? And how did the thieves get through the guard which had been placed around the sepulchre?

The question of the guards must also be raised with those who believe that the authorities stole the body (to prevent a hoax), or that the disciples took it (to support their claim that Christ was alive). There are some fatal objections to these theories. If the authorities stole the body, why did they not produce it, or at least say they had stolen it, when Peter was later boldly announcing the resurrection of Christ? That single piece of information would have destroyed in a moment the new movement that they regarded as so dangerous.

If the disciples stole it, why did they not say so when they were being tortured and killed for their belief in the resurrection? They could have saved their lives by saying that the resurrection was a cock-and-bull story which they themselves had invented. Instead they all continued to insist that the resurrection was a fact. If it was not, would not at least one of them have cracked, and have said differently?

And what shall we say of the grave-clothes that were left behind? Nobody intent on stealing the body, whatever their motive, would surely have left them in place. But there is more to it than that. The grave-clothes remained completely undisturbed. Round Christ's head had been a sort of turban. His body had been encircled with bandages. The body was gone, but this bandaging was in no way unfurled. It was as if the body had passed through it, and the weight of the spices wound into the grave-clothes made the whole thing resemble a collapsed cocoon. The turban for the head had fallen over and lay, still twirled, a few inches from the other wrappings.

These phenomena are inexplicable unless we accept the resurrection. Jesus' body acquired new powers and, as the Gospel narratives testify, became able to pass through solid objects. Our Lord did not need to roll back the stone to get out of the tomb. Angels rolled that back so that we could look *in*, and see that he was indeed risen from the dead. The undisturbed grave-clothes were enough to convince John that a resurrection had certainly taken place, and should be enough to convince us also.

After this, on ten separate occasions, the Lord was seen. These appearances were not hallucinations. These, as is well known, occur only after a long period of expectancy, and almost always in places associated with the deceased. But none of the disciples was expecting Jesus to rise! And the places where he was seen were very diverse, and by no means restricted to familiar haunts.

It is almost impossible to believe that the narratives of the resurrection appearances are invented. They are simple, unadorned, vivid and free from excess. Experienced lawyers assure us that these are the very features which characterize the testimony of truthful witnesses.

If we were inventing the stories, we would certainly have played down the doubts and fears of the disciples as they met the risen Lord. But the Gospels record these fully. We would also probably have included a graphic description of the Lord actually rising. But such a feature is entirely absent. Nobody witnessed the moment of resurrection.

But there is another point, and one which

I personally found very convincing when I first
seriously examined the claims of Christianity. It is
the fact that the records of the resurrection appearances are a hopeless jigsaw. It is almost impossible
to put them in order, and to work out what happened
when. If we were inventing the whole story, we
surely would have avoided this. We would have
made the whole chain of events coherent, and easy
to follow. As it is, the more an impartial reader
examines the endings of the four Gospels, the more
convinced he becomes that he is not reading a fabri-
cated tale. He is reading the truth.

In addition to all this, we must ask what it was
that changed Simon Peter from a man too terrified
to acknowledge Christ before a servant girl to a man
who preached with conquering boldness and pointed
application to the very people of Jerusalem who had
so shamefully treated his Lord. What changed James,
the Lord's half-brother, from an unrepentant unbeliever to a Christian of such steadiness that he
became one of the most important leaders of the
early church? The New Testament records that the
Lord Jesus Christ personally appeared to both men,
but those who do not believe in the resurrection must
find some other way to explain the transformation
of these two lives.

And what about the early church? How do we
explain its phenomenal growth and resilience? What
inspired and fired it, so that it grew despite all its
enormous difficulties and unrelenting opposition?
Can we believe that it was motivated by *nothing*?
The New Testament teaches that the early disciples
were moved to their world-wide ministry of evange-
lization and church-planting by one who had been
dead, but who had presented himself alive to them.
It says that by means of the ministry of the Holy

Spirit, they continued to enjoy Christ's company, even after his return to heaven — and that those who believed through their word entered into the same experience. Is that not a *better* explanation of the facts?

Is it not now time for you to forsake your own unbelief, and to receive the Scripture's testimony to the identity of Jesus Christ? But mental assent alone is not sufficient. Christ may be approached and *known.* Like Thomas, will you not now lay aside your doubts and confess to *Christ himself* what you have come to believe about him? And will you not also take heart from the words which follow?

'And Thomas answered and said to Him, "My Lord and my God!" Jesus said to him, "Thomas, because you have seen Me, you have believed. Blessed are those who have not seen and yet have believed" ' (John 20:28—29).

To pursue this subject:

   **Jesus of Nazareth — Who is He?* by Arthur Wallis. (Paperback, Christian Literature Crusade.)
   ***More than a Carpenter* by Josh MacDowall. (Paperback, Kingsway Publications.)
   ****The Incomparable Christ* by J. Oswald Sanders. (Paperback, Marshall, Morgan and Scott.)

6.
Was the cross really necessary?

We have spoken of the resurrection of Jesus Christ, but before that came his cross. After being mocked and cruelly flogged he was made to carry the heavy crossbeam of his cross along the dusty road which led from the city of Jerusalem to Golgotha, the place of a skull. As it was, his earlier suffering had so weakened him that he could not do it, and a passer-by was compelled to carry it for him.

By nine o'clock on that historic Friday morning our Lord had been crucified. Stripped naked, he was laid horizontally on the cross, his hands nailed to its crossbeam and his feet to its stem. As the cross was lifted vertically and dropped into its socket in the ground, every one of his bones was dislocated and his body shuddered in excruciating agony.

He hung there until late afternoon. The Jewish religious leaders passed by and mocked his shame, calling on him to prove his claims by coming down from the cross. The crown of thorns pressed heavily into his brow, the untended wounds on his back were probably soon filled with flies, while his hands and feet bled freely. Every time he let the weight of his body fall, the position his body was in made certain that he began to suffocate, while the nails in his hands began to tear the flesh. To breathe, our Lord had to push himself up into a more upright position, whereupon the whole weight of his body had to be borne by the nails through his feet. Who can tell the pain that he suffered? Exposed to the eastern heat, and overcome with a horrendous thirst, there was no comfort for his suffering. Crucifixion was a fiendish torture, guaranteeing the constant movement of the victim, for whom there was no relief, even for a short period. The Romans had developed it into a fine skill, and were able to secure victims in such a way that they often took days to die. The whole gruesome scene left the soldiers untouched. While the Son of God bled, they sat at his feet casting lots for his clothes.

Jesus Christ died the death normally reserved for the worst sort of criminal. The Roman world knew no greater shame than to die by crucifixion. It was the ultimate disgrace, and anybody who had a relative or friend executed in this way did his best to keep it a secret. But not so the early Christians. They *gloried* in Christ's cross! It was the very centre of their message, and they spoke of it everywhere. The cultured Greek-speaking people of the empire found the message foolish, and the Jews found it impossible to come to terms with the idea of a suffering Messiah and Saviour. But this did not deter the early believers. The cross of their Lord Jesus Christ meant more to them than anything else in the world. They spoke of it with evident euphoria, and all attempts to silence them failed miserably. The cry of Paul was the cry of them all: 'God forbid that I should glory except in the cross of our Lord Jesus Christ' (Galatians 6:14).

The whole world knows that the cross is the symbol of Christianity. Why is this? What happened there, which has filled so many with such amazement? The Romans crucified tens of thousands of people, almost all of whom have been forgotten. What was so special about the crucifixion at despised Golgotha that Friday? Why is it still remembered, not with a sense of shame, but with gratitude and affection? When we grasp the truths outlined in this chapter, all becomes clear. When our hearts as well as our heads understand these things, we too join the worshipping band who see Christ's crucifixion as the most important event in human history, and who are not surprised to learn that this cross is also the constant theme of heaven.

We are law-breakers
We start by remembering that the God of the Bible is the living and true God, who created all things from nothing, and to whom all men and women are answerable. All that he wants his creatures to know concerning him and their duty towards him is contained in the Scriptures. How can we remember all that they teach? We cannot, and therefore God has summarized what he expects of us in the Ten Commandments recorded in Exodus 20:1–17. These are a written repetition and summary of the law written by God into the human conscience. Unlike the temporary judicial laws of Old Testament Israel and the ceremonial laws which passed away at the death of Christ, this law is binding upon the whole human race for all time. It is binding upon me.

A poem taught to children is an easy way of remembering the ten words of God's moral law:

> You shall not have more gods than me;
> Before no image bow the knee;
> Take not the name of God in vain;
> Nor dare the Sabbath to profane.
>
> Give both your parents honour due;
> Take heed that you no murder do,
> Abstain from thoughts and words unclean;
> Nor steal though you are poor and mean;
> Nor make a wilful lie nor love it;
> What is your neighbour's do not covet.

Knowing the frailty of the human memory, our Lord Jesus Christ further summarized the demands which God makes upon us. He reduced them to just two sentences. Yet these two sentences in no way play down the seriousness of the law, but rather serve to emphasize it. He said, ' *"You shall love the Lord your God with all your heart, with all your soul, and with all your mind."* This is the first and great commandment. And the second is like it: *"You shall love your neighbour as yourself."* On these two commandments hang all the Law and the Prophets' (Matthew 22:37–40).

One reading of these brief sentences is enough to convince us that we have not kept the law of God. They fill us with shame. We have completely failed to love God as commanded. It is ourselves we have put first. We have equally failed to love our neighbour as ourselves. We have consistently loved ourselves *more* than those around us. The law is broken. It lies in pieces. We are a million miles from what God expects us to be. We try and compare ourselves favourably with others, but know that we cannot lift up our heads confidently before God and assure *him* that we are what he requires us to be. The Bible defines sin as 'lawlessness' (1 John 3:4), and is certainly right to teach that 'all have sinned and fall short of the glory of God' (Romans 3:23). We are in that number. We have broken through his law again and again. Whatever we are in our own eyes, we are *sinners* in his.

We are condemned – for God is just

Reading the Bible is a painful experience. It speaks to us so frankly about our condition. It tells us that if we had kept God's law, all would be well with us. We would be acceptable to the holy and just God of whom it speaks. We would be in his favour. There would be nothing between us. We would know him and enjoy him perfectly — just as we were created to do. Eternal life would be ours, for the Scriptures say about God's commandments that *'The man who does them shall live by them'* (Galatians 3:12).

Such teaching only serves to underline the awful situation we are in. We have *not* kept the law. All is *not* well. We are *not* acceptable to the eternal and living God. We are out of favour. What the ancient prophet said of Israel is also true of us: 'Your iniquities have made a separation between you and your God, and your sins have hid His face from you, so that He does not hear' (Isaiah 59:2). We are far, far away from him, and neither know him nor enjoy him. We have nothing to look forward to, except eternal condemnation, for *'Cursed is everyone who does not continue in all things which are written in the book of the law, to do them'* (Galatians 3:10).

Years ago I had a thought which made me very afraid. I was reflecting on the infinity of God, against whom I had sinned. It struck me that each offence against him was an infinite offence, because it was an offence against an infinite Person. My conscience wounded me as it had never done before. I knew that such an offence must be punished, for God is holy and cannot look upon sin. I came to see that the punishment must be infinite, because what other punishment would be appropriate and just for an *infinite* sin? My terrified heart came to understand what the Scriptures meant when they spoke of the eternal punishment of sinners in terms of 'perishing' (Romans 5:12; 6:23; John 3:16). Could any other word better convey the horror of being under his eternal condemnation? I had previously laughed at the idea of hell, but did so no longer. My heart was

solemnized. The eternal God was *angry* with me:
'For the wrath of God is revealed from heaven
against all ungodliness and unrighteousness of
men . . .' (Romans 1:18).

We cannot get back into God's favour by ourselves
It is a terrible thing to go through life knowing that
your Judge is against you. The thought filled me with
confusion. I had no peace. Only one thing mattered
to me — how could I get right with God? How could
I have my sins forgiven?

I looked at the Ten Commandments with despair.
They had shown me what I was like in God's eyes,
but gave me no hope of ever being right with him.
They proved to me that I had God as my enemy. His
law had been broken by *my* thoughts, *my* lips and *my*
hands. His justice rightly called for my eternal condemnation. What could I do? I could see little hope
of keeping the commandments in future, but even if
I did, what about the past? How could I make up for
that? God would not forget it. Indeed, 'God seeks
what has passed by' (Ecclesiastes 3:15). Even if my
future was perfect, the sins of the past remained an
affront to God. He sees past, present and future as
an open book before him. Nothing is hidden from his
eyes. However much I put things straight, I still
remained in his sight one who had infinitely sinned
against him. There was no escape. My damnation
was certain — and I knew that it was just.

In those days I did not know that God always
wounds us with his Word before he heals us by the
same Word. I had heard the gospel a thousand times,
I should imagine, but it never meant anything to me
until God's law cut me to pieces and brought me to
see myself as hopeless and helpless. I had to learn
that 'by the deeds of the law no flesh will be justified

in His sight, for by the law is the knowledge of sin' (Romans 3:20). Until I did, I was not ready to listen to the gospel with attention.

The word 'gospel' means 'good news'. I had known that since I was a toddler. But I did not realize what good news it was until I saw myself as a condemned sinner with no certain future other than that of screaming in hell, and also saw that I was totally unable, by my own power, to do anything about it. How wonderful it was in *that* situation to hear that although I cannot save myself, there is another who can! I had previously thought very little about Christ's cross. I did so now, for I heard that 'it pleased God by the foolishness of the message preached to save those who believe . . . we preach Christ crucified' (1 Corinthians 1:21, 23).

Do you know what it means to someone who sees that he is eternally lost and condemned to be told that there is hope for him because of what happened at Christ's cross? Do you know that sense of astonishment which such a person experiences when he hears someone announce, 'I am not ashamed of the gospel of Christ, for it is the power of God to salvation for everyone who believes'? (Romans 1: 16.) I had sometimes sniggered at those who had talked of being 'saved'. But once a person knows himself to be perishing, there is no theme which he wants to hear about more. He is impatient to be told how what happened at Golgotha almost 2000 years ago can possibly benefit a helpless sinner today.

God is love

We cannot understand the meaning of the cross unless we remember that God is love. He does not desire the punishment of any sinner. He says, 'I have no pleasure in the death of anyone who dies.' 'I take no pleasure in the death of the wicked, but rather that the wicked turn from his way and live' (Ezekiel 18:32; 33:11).

God's justice insists that the penalty demanded by his broken law should be paid. But it is also true that he 'is longsuffering toward us, not desiring that any should perish but that all should come to repentance' (2 Peter 3:9). The Bible reveals God's justice. It also reveals his grace. It tells us of our deserved condemnation. It also tells us that God 'desires all men to be saved and to come to the knowledge of the truth' (1 Timothy 2:4).

So it was, before the world began, he planned to send Christ to the cross to be a Saviour of perishing men and women. The cross was no accident. It was a wicked thing for God's creatures to murder his Son. Yet the event occurred because of the 'determined counsel and foreknowledge of God' (Acts 2:23). God rules the world in such a way that even the free acts of wicked people serve his purposes, and bring them to pass. We repeat — the cross was no accident. It was the very reason for Christ's coming into the world. He came to die. It was by the crucifixion of his Son that God planned to save those who could never save themselves. It was the supreme display of his love to perishing sinners.

This is how the Bible speaks of it: 'For God so loved the world that He gave His only begotten Son, that whoever believes in Him should not perish but have everlasting life.' 'In this is love, not that we loved God, but that He loved us and sent His Son to be the propitiation for our sins' (John 3:16; 1 John 4:10).

Christ's cross satisfies both God's justice and his love
All this is very well, but what actually *happened* at

Golgotha which secured the rescue and salvation of condemned law-breakers? It is not enough to speak of the cross as the supreme display of God's love to the perishing. We need to know in what way that cross has been able to do anything about their awful situation. A person conscious of the horror of his eternal destination is overcome with relief to hear that God takes no pleasure in his punishment, and that he has dealt with the situation by the death of his Son. But *how* did that shameful death accomplish anything for others?

The plain truth is this: the cross was a place of punishment. Jesus was punished there. He was punished physically, and we have already spoken of the horrors of crucifixion. But he was also punished spiritually. As an old writer put it, 'The soul of His suffering was the suffering of His soul.' He was cut off from God. This was why the sky went black and the world was covered with a supernatural darkness for three hours that day. God cannot look upon sin and at that moment Jesus was, in God's sight, the worst sinner who has ever lived. He made him who knew no sin to *be* sin (2 Corinthians 5:21). The one who was himself the eternal God was cut off from his Father. The place of the skull rang with the horrendous cry: 'My God, My God, why have You forsaken Me?' (Matthew 27:46.)

We must underline something which we learned in the last chapter, and which the Scriptures repeatedly stress. Jesus had no sins of his own. There was nothing to punish him for. Yet he *was* punished at the cross. What is the explanation?

In an earlier chapter we saw that death is God's curse upon sin. Jesus had no sins to be cursed for. There was no reason for him to die. But he did. Why? Why was the innocent Son of God both punished and cursed?

The answer is that he took the punishment due to others. He underwent the curse so that others might be delivered from it. He had nothing to die for, but died in the place of others. What was deserved by others, he took upon himself. He took their place. He substituted for them. *This* is what was happening at the cross.

This is not an explanation we are making up for ourselves. It is the unmistakable teaching of the Bible. We have already read that the Bible calls Jesus a 'propitiation'. This is not an everyday word, but is a most important word in Scripture. It means that Christ appeased the anger of God by taking it upon himself. The anger of God upon sin was poured out, but not on the sinners who deserved it. The righteous wrath of God, which should fall on every believer, fell instead on the Lord Jesus Christ, when he suffered on the cross. Our infinite sins cry out for infinite punishment. But the infinite Son of God bore that infinite anger that day at Golgotha.

Let us listen to how Paul put this truth. Writing to the Christian believers in Galatia, he said, 'Christ has redeemed us from the curse of the law, having become a curse for us; for it is written, *"Cursed is everyone who hangs on a tree"*' (Galatians 3:13). 'Redeemed' means 'released by the payment of a price'. Believers know that they have been released from the awful consequences of their sin — from the curse. The penalty which has to be paid by those who have broken the law of God was paid when Jesus hung on the cross.

Seven hundred years before he was born, the prophet Isaiah wrote of the death of Christ like this:

> 'But He was pierced through for our trans-
> gressions,

He was crushed for our iniquities;
The chastening for our well-being fell upon Him,
And by His scourging we are healed.
All of us like sheep have gone astray,
Each of us has turned to his own way;
But the Lord has caused the iniquity of us all
To fall on Him'   (Isaiah 53:5—6).

Christ's dying in our place means that God's justice has been perfectly satisfied. Justice demands that the penalty be paid, and it *has* been. But the cross also satisfies God's love. God may no longer justly exclude those who had their place taken by Jesus Christ. His anger against them has been poured out on their Substitute. The controversy is over. There is no punishment for them to bear.

Not only so, but just as God accepts Christ's death instead of theirs, he also accepts Christ's life instead of theirs. They are reckoned to be as he is — without fault. Without compromising his justice in any way, God freely embraces, welcomes and accepts all sinners who approach him on the basis of what Christ has done. The way back to God is open. Those who could never please him may now approach him without fear. Their sins have been atoned for. Their pardon is complete. Reckoned to their account is the righteousness of another. The God who never desired that any of them should perish has secured a way for them *not* to do so!

Therefore . . .
Those who wish to know God and to escape his fearful punishment must face the fact that Jesus Christ is their only hope. As we have seen, their own efforts will never be good enough to earn the favour of him who is *holy*. Every sin ever committed is an infinite

offence, and deserves God's everlasting anger. The
only life which has ever perfectly pleased him is
that of his Son. The only one fit to die in the place
of others was the same perfect person. Everybody
else had sins of his own to die for. No wonder that
the apostles said of Christ, 'Nor is there salvation in
any other, for there is no other name under heaven
given among men by which we must be saved'!
(Acts 4:12.)

But how do we enter into the benefits which the
Lord Jesus Christ has secured by his life, death and
resurrection? How do they become *ours*?

There are two things to do. Jesus announced them
at the very beginning of his public ministry: 'The
time is fulfilled, and the kingdom of God is at hand.
Repent and *believe* in the gospel' (Mark 1:15, italics
mine).

The apostle Paul went throughout the early world
preaching salvation through Christ. Here is his own
summary of his message: 'I kept back nothing that
was helpful to you, but declared it to you, and
taught you publicly and from house to house, testi-
fying to Jews, and also to Greeks, *repentance* toward
God and *faith* toward our Lord Jesus Christ' (Acts
20:20—21, italics mine).

To benefit from what Christ did for sinners at his
cross, we must repent and believe. Both are required,
and in fact cannot be separated.

Repentance means that we change our minds
about sin, and turn from it to God. We no longer
love the things he hates. We are ashamed that we
have displeased him for so long, and in so many
different ways. We see how we were made for him,
and how we have grieved him by living for ourselves.
We make up our mind to be like that no longer. We
resolve that, with his help, we will be different. In

future we will do all we can to please him. We hate our sins, because they brought the Lord Jesus Christ to the unspeakable sufferings of the cross. We turn away from them and put them behind our back.

This does not mean that we become perfect. Our lives will be filled with all sorts of failings until we die. We will not be perfect until the resurrection day. None the less, from the moment we repent, we have declared *war* on all sin in our lives. The Christian life begins with repentance, but such repentance also continues every day afterwards.

Faith means that we no longer hope to earn our way into God's favour. We abandon all hope of ever doing so. Instead we believe that all that is necessary for our salvation has been accomplished by Christ. There is nothing to add to what he has done. We believe that the life which God demands from us has been lived by him. We believe that the death which sinners deserve to die has been died by him. We believe that he is Lord, and that he is alive to guarantee the acceptance of all who come to God by him.

All this we believe in our heads. We are convinced of it. But there is more to faith than that. It is not just believing the truth *about* Christ, but actually trusting *him*. It involves an approach to him. Believing that he alone can rescue sinners from their damnation and secure their acceptance with God, I approach him and ask him to save *me*.

He is my only hope, so I call out to him. He is the only one I trust to bring me to God, so I pray to him to do so. My heart cries, 'God be merciful to me a sinner!' (Luke 18:13), and takes comfort from God's sure promise that '*"Whoever believes on Him will not be put to shame."* For there is no distinction between the Jew and Greek, for the same Lord over all is rich to all who call upon Him. For *"whoever*

calls upon the name of the Lord will be saved"'
(Romans 10:11—13).

From that moment my walk with God begins.
The road is different, and so is the destination. There
are countless difficulties and countless blessings
along the way. Everything is new. The change is not
my own doing. It was all brought about by the cross.
I can never again doubt that it was necessary, for
without it I would not be here.

To pursue this subject:

   *What the Scriptures teach by Ernest F. Kevan.
   (Paperback, Evangelical Press.)
   **The Atonement,* by John Murray. (Booklet,
   Presbyterian and Reformed Publishing Com-
   pany.)
   ***The Atonement,* by A. A. Hodge. (Paperback,
   Evangelical Press.)

7.
How long does it take to become a Christian?

At the close of our previous chapter we learned how to become a Christian. It is worth stressing that a Christian is something you *become*. Nobody is born a Christian. Nobody is a Christian because his parents were. Nor is someone to be considered a Christian simply because he is a citizen of a 'Christian' country. True Christians can all look back on a time when they were *not* Christians — as the New Testament repeatedly makes clear.

Great issues hang on this question of whether you have become a Christian or not. In fact, *eternal* issues hang on it. Let us state the matter plainly. Only those who are Christians (in the sense the Bible uses the word) inherit eternal life. People who do not become Christians remain cut off from God, and as long as they remain as they are, they are perishing and bound to bear the infinite punishment which their sins justly deserve.

This chapter, then, deals with a question of vital importance. Only those who have become Christians will be acquitted and received by God at the last day. All others will be turned away. Unless you have become a Christian in this life, this is your certain destiny. It is therefore extremely important to know how long it takes to become one.

Did you do quadratic equations at school? If so, you will remember that every quadratic equation has two correct answers, and your teacher demanded that you state both. For example, the answer to a particular equation might be either -4.3 or 4.3.

There can hardly be anything more different than a minus number and a plus number, and yet both would be right. The answer has not been properly stated unless both numbers are written as the solution.

It is just the same with the question now before us. There are two answers, and both are required if the question is to be answered accurately. It is not enough to say that it takes a long time to become a Christian, or to answer that it takes only a moment. Accuracy demands that we say both. If we do not, we shall have said less than the truth.

The best way we can explain this is by studying two conversions which are recorded in the Acts of the Apostles. As we examine each of them we will underline four points — four points which are true of *every* conversion. We will very quickly see that it takes *a long time* to become a Christian. We will also see that it takes only *a moment*. Our study will clearly reveal why it is essential to give both answers, and how it is possible.

As most of the readers of this book are probably Gentiles, I have chosen the conversion of two Gentiles for our study. One was a black man from Ethiopia, and the other a white Roman in Palestine. There were vast differences between them in background, occupation, social position and experience. They became Christians in vastly different circumstances. Yet their conversions had four common factors. Two thousand years of church history have served only to increase the diversity of those who come to Christ. The four factors have not altered. They remain the unchanging features of every true conversion.

The Ethiopian eunuch

We have mentioned the Bible a great deal in this book, and quoted from it many times. Would you now like to take down your own copy, and to open it at the Acts of the Apostles? There, in chapter 8, from verses 26 to 39, we have the easy-to-read narrative of the conversion of a eunuch from Ethiopia.

This eunuch was in a position of great trust in the court of Candace, Queen of Ethiopia at that time. He 'had charge of all her treasury'. He was the equivalent there of our Chancellor of the Exchequer. The record is of the conversion of a very prominent and important court official.

Somehow or other (we do not know how), there in distant Ethiopia this eunuch developed an interest in the God whose temple was found in Jerusalem. Numerous deities were worshipped in his homeland, but they did not satisfy him. His interest was in the invisible God of the universe who was proclaimed by the Jews. He therefore set out on the long and hazardous journey by chariot to the distant Jerusalem temple, that he might worship him.

What transpired during his visit to Jerusalem we also do not know. We do know that while there he succeeded in obtaining at least part of the Old Testament Scriptures. His visit obviously did nothing to dampen his interest in the God of Israel for, during his journey home, he set himself to read the prophet Isaiah. By the time he had reached the desert road near Gaza he was already up to chapter 53! The difficulties of the book had obviously not deterred him from his spiritual quest, and he read on regardless. Not only was he reading, however, but he was asking questions concerning the meaning of the book. He was particularly interested in knowing who Isaiah was talking about in the remarkable chapter before

him. The passage spoke of God's Servant, who was
suffering dreadfully — not for his own sins, but for
the sins of others. Was Isaiah writing about himself,
or of some other person — and, if so, whom? In the
chariot sat a man who was filled with interest in the
Word of God.

The first point we should notice about the conversion of this eunuch is that *God prepared him*. Nobody can have a sincere, lasting and searching interest
in the things of God unless God is already at work in
his life. The Bible teaches that all our minds and
consciences are spoiled by sin. They are blinded and
twisted. Left to ourselves, we cannot so much as
desire or seek God. We are spiritually dead, and
unable to move ourselves in a God-ward direction.
Yet here was a man seeking God — hard! He had
travelled hundreds of miles and was working away
at an extremely difficult Old Testament book. God
had obviously touched his heart and had given him
spiritual interest. He was to become a Christian
because God had taken this initiative in his life.

The second point we notice is that *a servant of
God met him*. Seventy miles or more to the north,
in the city of Samaria, the evangelist Philip was
preaching with great success. People were turning
out in their hundreds to hear him and whole communities were turning to Christ as a result. It was
at this point that Philip received a message from God,
telling him to leave Samaria and to go down to the
desert road which leads from Jerusalem to Gaza.

He set off at once, and arrived at the appointed
spot in the middle of nowhere. Shortly afterwards,
along came a chariot. Very probably there were
several chariots in convoy. As they went by, the
Spirit of God said to Philip, 'Go near and overtake
this chariot,' indicating one in particular. Philip did

so and had to run to catch it up. As he jogged along-side it, he was amazed to hear the person inside reading aloud (as they do in the East) from the Word of God!

Philip asked the stranger, 'Do you understand what you are reading?'

'How can I', he replied, 'unless someone guides me?' And he invited Philip to jump up and sit with him in the chariot.

The eunuch now took his opportunity to ask the question which had been troubling him: 'I ask you, of whom does the prophet say this, of himself or of some other man?'

And beginning at the very same Scripture verse, the servant of God preached Jesus to him. The man whom God had prepared had met a servant of God!

What followed brings out our third point. *The Saviour was presented to him from the Scriptures.* Beginning at the chapter and verse which the eunuch was reading, Philip began to explain. If you have never done so, it is worth reading Isaiah 53 at this point. It is a chapter about sin. It is a chapter about those who have committed iniquity in the sight of God and who are therefore not at peace with him. It is about men and women who, like sheep, have gone astray from God. It explains that although we have all turned like this to our own way, 'the Lord has caused the iniquity of us all to fall on *Him*' (Isaiah 53:6).

The chapter declares that 'He was pierced through for our transgressions, He was crushed for our iniqui-ties; the chastening for our well-being fell upon Him, and by His scourging we are healed' (Isaiah 53:5). It speaks of somebody innocently suffering in the place of the wicked, and removing their wickedness by bearing its penalty. It is a chapter about God's Son, the Lord Jesus Christ, dying on the cross in the place of sinners. It explains how the coming of Jesus Christ, and his dying upon the cross, is the *only* way by which men and women can be put right with God.

So three things have happened. A man prepared by God has met his servant, who has explained to him who Jesus Christ is, and what he has done. The fourth point to notice concerning the eunuch's conversion is that *the Holy Spirit worked in him.* Nobody can truly believe that Jesus Christ is Lord unless the Holy Spirit has worked in his mind, affections and will, and brought him to that conviction (1 Corinthians 12:3). Nobody can commit himself to Christ, relying on him for his acceptance with God, unless the Holy Spirit gives him such faith.

As the chariot trundled along, with Philip and the eunuch doing Bible study in the back, the road passed a small brook or pond. The eunuch looked up and noticed it. 'Look!' he exclaimed, 'Water! What is there to stop me being baptized?'

Being baptized was (and still is) a public declaration that the person concerned had become a Christian. Philip's reply to the request was 'If you believe with all your heart, you may.'

'I believe!' said the eunuch, 'I believe that Jesus Christ is the Son of God.'

The eunuch had come to see who Jesus Christ was and what he had done, and was willing to stake himself upon what he knew. The Holy Spirit had worked in his mind and there, in the chariot, he had become a Christian!

How long did it take? God took the initiative and saw the whole process through. But God is the unchangeable God. If he works in a person's life, it is because he has decided to do so. But if God decided one day to do something which the day before he had *not* decided to do, he would be a changing God. He would be something one day, but something different the next. This is impossible, and we must therefore draw the conclusion that his decision to work in the eunuch's life was an *eternal* decision. It was something he had chosen to do *for as long as he had been God.*

How long does it take to become a Christian? A long time! It was God's eternal purpose to save this eunuch, and everything in his earlier life would have served God's plan to bring him at last to salvation. Years and years went by until the moment of conversion came — the moment when the eunuch would rest all his hopes of acceptance with God upon the Lord Jesus Christ. His becoming a Christian took a long time! His becoming a Christian took a moment!

When he got into his chariot at Jerusalem he was not a Christian. Nor was he when Philip got in, somewhere on the desert road. He was still not a Christian when Philip explained the lengthy chapter of Isaiah. But by the time he saw the water, he was! At a precise instant, at an unknown spot on a deserted road, he came to rest on Christ alone for his standing with God. Under God's direction the whole of his life had been leading up to that moment. On the Gaza road he passed from darkness to light, and was delivered from the power of Satan and came to God. He became what God had planned him to be. It was still something he *became* — and he became it in a moment.

Cornelius
Our second story is found a couple of pages further on in our Bible, and occupies the whole of Acts

chapter 10. It is a well-known passage of the New
Testament and concerns Cornelius, a Roman centurion, who was stationed at Caesarea on the Mediter-
ranean coast of Palestine. He was almost certainly
brought up on the mainland of Italy and schooled
in its pagan rites and idolatry. Such a Roman officer
would normally have been detested by the Jews,
who longed for release from the Roman yoke, and
the establishment of an independent Jewish state.
But not so Cornelius. He was known as 'a just man,
one who fears God and has a good reputation among
all the nation of the Jews' (Acts 10:22). This devout
man's fear of God was shared by his household. He
was loved because of his generous gifts to the poor,
and because he was constantly at prayer to God
(10:2).

What we have here, then, is a man born and bred
in a pagan environment, who became truly interested
in the God of Scripture, and concerned both to know
and to please him.

Cornelius was religious. He prayed. He gave gifts
to those in need. But he was not yet a Christian. We
must not think that being a Christian is anything to
do with such observances. Yet his search for God was
sincere, and we must once more stress that there can
be no such earnest searching without God himself
being involved in the process. Wherever hearts truly
seek him, it is because *he* has set them to seek. This
is why we can be certain that those who intently
seek him will surely find him. Setting hearts to seek
him is the first thing he does in the life of a person
that he intends should know him. The initiative in
every conversion is God's. Cornelius was going to
find him, because *God prepared him*. What other
explanation can there be when we find a sinner
yearning and burning to know the true and living

God? The heart of someone spiritually dead cannot be the source of sustained spiritual interest, so the source must be *another*!

One afternoon at about 3 o'clock, while Cornelius was praying, an angel appeared to him! He told Cornelius to send for Simon, surnamed Peter, who was currently about thirty-five miles down the coast, at Joppa. He could be found lodging at the home of Simon the tanner, by the seaside.

This message from God enforces our first point. God had prepared Cornelius. Now events were being set in motion by which God's servant was going to meet him. Cornelius immediately acted on the divine message and sent two household servants and a devout soldier to find Peter as directed. On Day 1 he sent them. On Day 2 they travelled, arrived and stayed the night. On Day 3 they duly journeyed back with Simon Peter and six of his Christian friends. On Day 4 they arrived at Cornelius' home, where all his close friends and relatives were expectantly waiting. They had gathered at Cornelius' invitation, and were ready to hear all the words which God had commanded Peter to speak. The centurion became a Christian not simply because God prepared him, but because *a servant of God met him.*

At this point *the Saviour was presented to him scripturally.* Peter stood before the excited company, and began to explain all about the Lord Jesus Christ. An outline of what he said is preserved for us in verses 34 to 43. He explained about the deity of Christ, and that he is Lord of all. God himself has come to our planet as Jesus of Nazareth. Peter told them about Jesus' life and his miracles and how he 'went about doing good and healing all who were oppressed by the devil, for God was with Him'. The one who was God himself was *sent* by God, and God was *with* him! Peter did not evade mentioning such mysteries, but rather emphasized them to display even more of the wonder of the person of Christ.

He also mentioned Jesus' cross, and how he had been done to death and buried. He spoke boldly of Christ's resurrection, and how he himself was numbered among those who had seen the risen Saviour! Indeed, he had eaten and drunk with Christ after his rising from the dead! He proclaimed that it is *this* Christ that God has ordained to be the Judge of the living and the dead. He pressed upon Cornelius, and all those present, that all the prophets witnessed that through Christ everyone who believed in him would receive remission of sins.

Peter's message, then, was about their sin and their need to have it forgiven and forgotten. He told them that only God, in Jesus Christ, is the Saviour of sinners. The death, resurrection and exaltation of Christ were the very centre of his preaching. Peter was a very different preacher from Philip, with a very different congregation. But the message was the same.

During Peter's preaching a remarkable thing happened. *The Holy Spirit worked* in Cornelius — and not only in him, but also in his relatives and friends. As Peter spoke, the Holy Spirit fell, and all who heard were persuaded of the truth of the gospel. Not only so, but a remarkable sign was given. Peter had been accompanied to Caesarea by six Jewish Christian friends. They needed convincing that the gospel was not restricted to the Jews, but was for Gentiles, too. So it was that all who heard Peter were given the miraculous ability to speak fluently foreign languages which they had never learned — precisely the same supernatural phenomenon which believing Jews had received years before, ten days after Christ's ascension. Shortly afterwards Cornelius and his household and friends were baptized. They had become Christians!

It took a long time for Cornelius to become a Christian. It was the providence of God that brought him across the sea to Palestine, and into contact with the Jewish religion. It was God himself who gave him his persistent interest in knowing the God of Scripture for himself. As we have seen, it was God that brought Peter to preach the gospel to him, and it was God who, by his Holy Spirit, entered his life while the gospel was being preached. A process of years ended that day in Caesarea. If God had not planned it in eternity, he certainly would not have done it in time. Yet Cornelius passed from being a man seeking to a man found in a moment. It takes a long time, but only an instant, to become a Christian!

The birth of a baby
We can further illustrate this point by asking how long it takes for a baby to be born. There is the conception, there is the period of gestation and finally there is the moment of birth (when usually there is a midwife present). At last the baby is on public view!

It is the same with the spiritual birth which brings people into the spiritual realm. There is the conception in the plan of God, there are the years when God is secretly at work in the life and then there is the moment when the person becomes a Christian — usually with the assistance of a 'midwife'. It is only after this that there is a new Christian for others to see. Even at this point he is only a spiritual babe, who is liable to fall and to make many mistakes, and who needs lots of care and cherishing. At this stage he understands very little, is not very strong, can only take food which is specifically prepared for him and cannot get his teeth into anything for himself. But he is alive — spiritually alive — having been born again. His weakness does not suggest that he is not a true Christian, but only that he is new to spiritual things. Fed with the right food and surrounded by family care, he grows and becomes stronger, until at last he takes on something of the likeness of his Parent and becomes a man or woman of God. It takes a long time to become a Christian, yet it takes only a moment. It also takes a long time to become a *strong* Christian.

May I apply these things to you, and tell you that it is no accident that you are reading this book and this chapter. God's providence rules the world, and all things everywhere serve his purpose. It is possible that you are one of those whom God is preparing for salvation, and that reading this book is part of the process by which he will bring you to the moment when you personally trust the Lord Jesus Christ. Quite possibly you think that the decision to read this chapter was entirely your own. But God rules the world in such a way that even the free decisions of men and women bring to pass his purposes. Who is to know whether or not *God has prepared you*?

Cold print is a poor substitute for personal conversation, and yet it is a means which God has been pleased to use again and again. Books often go where none of God's servants has ever yet set foot. Many men and women will read a book about the things of God who, for one reason or another, will never speak about these things. I have written these chapters trying to be as faithful a servant of God as I can. You have read what I have written. *A servant of God has met you.*

By reading of the conversions of the eunuch and Cornelius *the Saviour has been presented to you scripturally.* Do you see what those two men saw when God's Word was opened to them? Seeing themselves as lost and condemned in God's sight, they repented and cast themselves upon the only one who could do anything for them — the Lord Jesus Christ, who died and rose to save believing sinners. They put no trust in their religion, or their prayers, or their dignity and social position. They saw that perishing sinners have no other hope than Jesus Christ. With a limited understanding, but none the less knowing that his power to save is tied up with his glorious person and his cross and resurrection, they came to trust him and entered into the favour of God.

Whatever you think of yourself, will you not now do the same? The invitation to do so is free and without reservation. No one who calls on Christ has ever been turned away, or will ever be so. Invisibly present by his Spirit, he receives all who come to him. He both commands and invites you to flee to him for refuge. He has borne the penalty for all who come to him in this way. Not to come is the worst sin of all, and certain to receive the worst punishment. But if you will cast yourself upon Christ, your sins will be pardoned, and a perfect righteousness reckoned to your account. You will be welcomed by God as his own child, and assured of his favour throughout both time and eternity. To embrace Christ in this way would be the supreme proof that *the Holy Spirit has worked in you.*

If you do this, you will have become a Christian. You will then be able to look back over your past life, and to see a thousand details which have jig-sawed together to bring you to this point in your

life. You will have become a Christian in a moment.
Yet you will be the first to admit that it took a long
time!

To pursue this subject:

   *Men of Purpose, by Peter M. Masters. (Paperback,
   Wakeman.)
  **How shall I go to God? by Horatius Bonar.
  (Paperback, Baker Book House.)
 ***A New Birth, by J. C. Ryle. (Paperback, Baker
 Book House.)

8.
Does it really matter what I believe?

There are many people today who say that it does not really matter what we believe. 'After all,' they say, 'all religions are very much the same. There is not a lot to choose between them. One is as good as the next. Who is to say what God is like? And as long as your religion satisfies *you*, that is all that matters.'

Quite recently I was in a home where some of the children went to church, while other children in the same family went each week to the mosque. The parents were quite unperturbed. 'It is all for God,' they said, 'so surely it does not matter whether they worship him in one building or the other.'

The Bible knows nothing of this sort of thinking. It insists that the truths it proclaims are in a class of their own. They cannot be put in a class with any other beliefs — not even at the head of the class. Biblical Christianity does not claim to be the *best* religion, but the one and only *true* religion. It declares that all other beliefs are false.

All religions contain elements of truth
This is not to say that *everything* which non-Christians believe is wrong. Every other religion contains elements of truth. Indeed, it would be strange if they did not. Man was created a religious being, and this immediately marked him out as different from the animals. His original religion was the true religion. But very shortly afterwards man

walked out on God and became corrupted. However, he retained his sense of God, although he no longer enjoyed personal fellowship with him. He continued to be a religious creature, but inevitably his religion was now different. It, too, shared in the corruption of sin.

Every religion in the world is a corruption of that original true religion. It would be surpassingly strange, would it not, if each one were so corrupted that not one shred of truth remained in it? As we have seen in several previous chapters, man still knows a good deal about God. It would be exceedingly surprising if the truths which he still knows were not in some way reflected in the forms of worship which he still keeps up.

So it is that almost all religions share a large number of common features. For example, every religion believes in a being who is greater than the worshipper. He believes in something other than himself which is greater than himself. Almost all religions also believe in some future existence for men and women. They cannot accept that death is the end. There is not total agreement as to what lies beyond. Some believe in reincarnation, and others hold to a spirit existence. But the underlying conviction of a future beyond what this world offers is very widespread indeed.

Religion everywhere has an outward form. There is some sort of organization, and some sort of service or cult to attend. Each one has its own rites and ceremonies. Some form of gathering together is expected. All religions have a concept of prayer, some form of sacrifice and nearly always some convictions about giving. There is also always an insistence on a code of morality — something which is recognized as 'good behaviour'. Some acts and thoughts are 'good' while others are 'bad'. There is not perfect agreement about which is which, but the very idea that a person may not act exactly as he pleases is common to all religions everywhere.

The Bible admits that there are these elements of truth in all religions. But this in no way lessens its bold assertion that it, and it alone, proclaims the one and only true religion, and that all other systems of belief, without exception, are essentially false.

Why is this? It is the one true religion because it alone has a true book — the 'sacred books' of other religions are misled and misleading. It alone proclaims the only true God — all other 'gods' are the invention of men's minds and are therefore idols. It points to the only true Saviour — every other so-called 'saviour' leads men and women to destruction. It reveals the only true morality — no other system of belief reveals what true holiness is and gives the necessary incentive to seek it. In short, if men and women believe any other way, they are in deep and eternal trouble.

The only true book
Let us take these points one by one. Most of the great religions of the world have sacred books — but Christianity alone has a true one. Of course we admit that the sacred books of the world contain wisdom. Some of them contain great wisdom. But at the end of the day it has to be said that, however great their wisdom, it is but the wisdom of men and women and is therefore fallible and imperfect.

The great exception is the religion of the Jews — Judaism. The Jews have the Old Testament, and therefore have thirty-nine of the sixty-six books which have been breathed out by God. But although they have in their hands two-thirds of what God has

caused to be written, they do not come to the truth.
This is partly because they reject the Messiah proclaimed in the pages they have; partly because they
do not have the total picture, rejecting, as they do,
the books of the New Testament; and partly because
to this day they have a veil over their understanding
when they read the books they have (2 Corinthians
3: 14—15).

Only Christianity has in its possession the one true
book — the inerrant and infallible Bible. We saw in
chapter 2 that the Bible is a book which can be
trusted, and that this is because it is the Word of
God. We should not overlook the relationship that
exists between this book and the Lord Jesus Christ.
It says of him that he is the truth (John 14:6). *He*
says of it, that it is the truth (John 17:17). It follows,
therefore, that whoever does not have the Bible and
does not believe it is incapable of coming to the
truth. Equally, wherever people *have* come to him
who is the truth, they have first come to submit to
the teachings of the Bible about him. Christ and the
Bible stand or fall together. By his Spirit, he is its
author; it is by his testimony that its integrity is
assured, and he is its constant theme. There is no
hope of anyone who neglects the Bible coming to
God's appointed Saviour.

Of all books in the world, the Bible alone has
been breathed by God. It alone is the true Word
from God to this world. Of all beliefs, biblical
Christianity alone is rooted in it. To believe anything else is to be certainly astray.

The only true God
The teaching of the entire Bible is that the God
who has revealed himself in it is *God alone*. There
is no other true God. There is but one alone — the

living God of Scripture. 'Thou alone art God,' wrote David (Psalm 86:10). It is this simple fact which gives God the moral right to command, 'You shall have no other gods before Me' (Exodus 20:3).

This God is unique, not in some respects, but in all. He is one, and yet there are three who are God — without there being three gods. Each Person of the Godhead is the whole of God, and is God in his own right. Each is equal. Each is eternal. And yet the Father is not the Son; the Son is not the Holy Spirit, and the Holy Spirit is not the Father. They are distinct, and have their own personal properties. The Father begets the Son, and sends the Spirit. The Son is begotten of the Father, and sends the Spirit from the Father. The Spirit proceeds from the Father and the Son, and acts for them. Within the Persons of the Godhead there is an order which in no way affects their equality.

This 'doctrine of the Trinity', as it is called, is an unfathomable mystery. It is a mystery taught nowhere else but in the Bible. Should we neglect or ignore the Bible, we would remain ignorant of the true nature of the Godhead. The Hindus have three principal gods, but no conception of the oneness of God. The Moslems believe in only one god, but have no understanding that there are three who are God. That God is *triune* is a truth discoverable only from the Scriptures. When we look anywhere else for the truth about him, we are misled.

The God of the Bible is perfect. His perfection shines in everything to do with him. We have all seen light shone through a prism and emerging as all the colours of the rainbow. So it is with the perfection of God. His perfection shines in many colours. All his attributes are but displays of this perfection. Everything that can be said about him is perfect. He has a perfect being. He is perfect in wisdom, in power, in holiness, in goodness, in justice and in truth. How unlike the gods of other religions! How different from the lustful, arbitrary and selfish gods of the ancient myths! How different from the gods of polytheistic religions today, who must have many gods, for each one is imperfect in some point or other!

God is not like anything which the human mind can imagine. He possesses absolute moral perfection. He cannot lie or do any wickedness (Numbers 23: 19; Job 34:10). Such is the majesty of his purity that even the sinless creatures that surround his throne cannot look upon him, but cry to each other with never-dying amazement, 'Holy, Holy, Holy, is the Lord of hosts . . .' (Isaiah 6:3).

We see God's perfection most clearly when we consider his justice and his love. Some religions, such as those which believe in reincarnation, preach justice without mercy. If my performance in this life is of the required standard, I will be promoted in the next incarnation. If it is not, I will be demoted. This justice applies right across the board and there is no escape from it for anyone.

On the other hand, there are those who preach mercy without justice. In this category we must put the vast majority of those who occupy 'Christian' pulpits. They teach that, however you live, God will accept you. He is put across as a naive and celestial grandfather, who turns a blind eye to everything. He forgives without any consideration of the fact that his broken law demands that a penalty should be paid.

God knows nothing of justice without mercy, or of mercy without justice. He is perfect in both attributes, and can compromise neither. His Son died for sinners, because justice demanded that the penalty for breaking the law should be paid. Yet Jesus died for *sinners*, because God's love demanded that a way of salvation should be opened for those who, left to themselves, could never escape the righteous anger of an offended God.

'Towering o'er the wrecks of time' stands the cross of Calvary, where God's justice and mercy met, and kissed in sweet embrace. That cursed place declares to the world that God is perfect in his justice, and sin must therefore be punished. It also declares that God is love, and the way back to him has been opened for sinners, because he, in the person of his Son, has borne the penalty for all believers. There is uncompromised justice! There is unspoiled love! There is the supreme display of the perfection of God!

The only true Saviour
It matters then very much what we believe. If we turn our back on the Bible, we have turned our back on the only true book that there is, and therefore on the way of salvation that it reveals. If we seek after other gods, we have turned away from the only God that really exists. If we try to secure acceptance with God any other way than by the Saviour he has sent, we have walked away from the only way by which we may come to know him, whom to know is life eternal.

There is no other way to be saved than through the Lord Jesus Christ, and it is the supreme example of folly to try. Men and women cannot save themselves. Salvation is the work of the triune God — the Father, the Son and the Holy Spirit. 'The Father has sent the Son as Saviour of the world' (1 John 4:14). It is the Holy Spirit who, in our experience, brings us to faith in him. But the work of accomplishing salvation was done by God the Son. This was why, before his birth, the angel announced to Joseph, 'You shall call His name JESUS, for He will save His people from their sins' (Matthew 1:21).

There are two important truths which we must remember about the saving work of Christ. The first is that *Jesus saves completely*. The other is that *only Jesus saves*. In other words, he does not need the assistance of anyone or anything else — of religion, of our good deeds, of Mary, of the 'saints', or of anything else whatever. There is no need of any other Saviour, nor is there any place for one.

Who is this Jesus Christ? We have answered this in chapter 5. But here we draw attention to the fact that the Bible presents him as the Prophet who alone teaches the truth about how we may be put right with an angry God. He is the Priest who is himself alone the sufficient and perfect sacrifice for sinners, and who is evermore alive to intercede for them, and to bear up their cause in heaven. He is the King who conquers the stubborn wills of his enemies, and who brings them to submit to the teachings of the gospel. Once they have come to faith, he rules them by his Word and Spirit and defends them against all their enemies. Not one of them fails to arrive at the destination he has prepared for them.

Jesus Christ alone is a perfect Saviour. This being so, there can never be any place for any other saviour. This is why he announced to the world, 'I am the way, the truth, and the life. No one comes to the Father except through Me' (John 14:6). This is why Paul wrote, 'For there is one God and one Mediator between God and men, the Man Christ Jesus' (1 Timothy 2:5). This is why Peter preached, 'Nor is there salvation in any other, for there is no other name under heaven given among men by which we must be saved' (Acts 4:12).

He is a *perfect* Saviour! The Bible reveals how he saves from the guilt of sin and from its penalty. He breaks its power in the lives of those who trust him, and will at last remove them from its very presence. He brings them to a true knowledge of God, and because of the life that he lived on earth, a perfect righteousness is credited to their account. This guarantees their unreserved acceptance by God. At his second coming he will raise them from the dead, and they will be perfectly holy. By his power, the everlasting life which they will enjoy then has actually been begun *now*.

All these things flow to men and women only through Jesus Christ. There is no hope of receiving them any other way. Without Christ there is no hope. It matters, then, *very much* what you believe.

The only true morality
As we believe, so we behave. The convictions which we nurse in our hearts govern our words and our actions. To put it in more sophisticated language — morality is rooted in religion. It is a fact that every religion on earth instructs its adherents to behave in a certain way.

It is the beliefs which a person has in his mind which bring him to decide whether a thing is 'right' or 'wrong'. As it happens, we are quickly coming to the point in the West where most people no longer have any clear beliefs. Deeply held convictions are becoming a thing of the past. How then do most people decide what is acceptable behaviour, and what is not? By and large, they make other people their standard. If other people do it, it is 'all right'. If not, then it ought not to be done, or should be considered very seriously first. What 'everybody' is doing is 'O.K.'. This is the religion of the hour. It is the deification of man.

Against this modern view of morality, God speaks. As our Creator and Judge he makes it clear that *he* requires something of us. On the basis of what his own character is like, he calls some things 'right', and others 'wrong'. His character never changes, so nor do his standards. What he calls right is *always* right, and what he calls wrong is *always* wrong. The standards are absolute and are not open to negotiation. And they are the standards by which we will all be judged.

Unless a person knows what God requires, he has no hope whatever of living in a way which pleases him. This is why it matters *very much* what we believe. People who have beliefs about personal behaviour which do not coincide with what he has said will be unspeakably ashamed and confounded when they stand before him in judgement.

What *does* God command his world? Love! But what is love? 'Love,' he replies, 'is the fulfilment of the law' (Romans 13:10).

God is love. This is why he commands men and women, who were originally made in his image, that they should be the same. They are to love God and, because they do, they are to love their neighbour — those made in the image of God. How they are to love God is expressed in the first four of the Ten Commandments, and how they are to love their neighbour in the next six (Exodus 20:1—17). Man can never be God. But his behaviour is to be *godly*. The pattern for all his behaviour is to be God himself. This is why Jesus said, 'Be perfect, just as your Father in heaven is perfect' (Matthew 5:48).

At this point Christianity stresses something

which no other religion on earth emphasizes. It is not sufficient to obey the letter of the commands which God gives. The spirit of the commands must also be kept. For example, abstaining from adultery does not simply mean that we do not commit the physical act. The command is broken when the thought of adultery is enjoyed. Obedience to the command means not even doing it in the *heart*. It is not enough to abstain from the act. The whole spirit of the person must be against it (see Matthew 5:27—32). There is more to law-keeping than putting right our outward behaviour. It requires a revolution in the whole personality. Those who do not stress this are a million miles from the morality which God demands.

It was to this point that Jesus was referring when he said, 'Unless your righteousness exceeds the righteousness of the scribes and Pharisees, you will by no means enter the kingdom of heaven' (Matthew 5:20). The religious groups of his day had a very strict code of outward behaviour. It enabled them to keep to the finest letter of the law, while very often ignoring its spirit completely. As long as the outward action was right, they did not give much attention to the heart and affections. Jesus declared that this was not the true morality demanded by God. Something much more stringent was required. Outward observance was simply not enough.

The Ten Commandments are still in force, as we saw in chapter 6. Keeping them in the right spirit would mean that our whole being would be taken up in love for God and for those around us. Nothing less is the morality which God expects from us.

Other religions say, 'Here are the commandments; keep them if you can.' The Bible says, 'Here are the commandments; but face it — you cannot keep them.

God demands that you should, but it is impossible to keep them in the way that he requires. But as God preaches his gospel through his servants and offers forgiveness through his Son, he also promises to those who call upon his Son a new heart and a new spirit. All sinners who flee to the Saviour find that new covenant promise to be true. They find that they become people who inwardly delight in God's law. They do not keep it as they should, and yet they long to do so. They love it. Their greatest desire is to love God and their neighbour as they should. They sincerely desire to spend their days pleasing him.'

Other religions say, 'Do these things and our god will have mercy upon you.' Christianity says, 'When God has mercy upon you, he will empower you to live increasingly in the way which pleases him.' One makes obedience the condition of receiving mercy. The other shows that receiving mercy is the beginning of a true obedience. These points of view are opposites. Those who believe wrongly must for ever be misled in this area. They put the cart before the horse. They stand the relationship of mercy to obedience on its head. It *does* matter what you believe!

Other religions say, 'Get this question of right and wrong sorted out, and there may be hope for you.' Christianity says, 'Come to the living God of mercy, through Christ. Then, and then only, will you have both power and incentive to live differently. You will love, because you yourself were loved first. You will live differently, because it is the only appropriate way of expressing your gratitude to the one who delivered you. Not only so, but he who forgave your sin has broken its power over you. For the very first time, living differently

is a real possibility and no longer just a vain hope.'
This emphasis makes Christianity different from
every other religion which has ever existed. It stands
unique.

It matters very much
Does it really matter what I believe? Yes, very much.
For unless I believe biblical Christianity I will have
spurned the only book where God authoritatively
speaks, the only God there is, the only person who
can save sinners and the only way of living which is
acceptable to him.

And it is to this God that I will answer at last.
I will stand at the last day before the one who gave
to the world his inspired Word and who has revealed
himself in it. I will be judged by the one who sent
his Son into the world. The standard of judgement
will be none other than the divine law which I considered to be no different from other codes. That
day will declare the immensity of such sin. It will
be seen as an infinite wickedness. And I will not be
able to offer any excuse. The real reason for my
failure to submit to what God has revealed will be
seen to be self-will and stubbornness. I will know
what it means to be condemned justly, and to perish
eternally. It will be the day of damnation, and the
abandonment of all hope. Lost in this life, I will be
lost for ever. I will spend all eternity pondering *how
much* it mattered what I believed.

But that day of judgement has not yet arrived.
There is still time to change my mind and to change
my direction. There is still time to forsake all other
hopes and to heed the Saviour's invitation to come
to him. There is still time to confess my folly and
to cast all my hopes on the one I have neglected
for so long. The cost and difficulty of living for

him in this present world will be more than compen-
sated for when I hear him say to me, 'Come, you
blessed of my Father, inherit the kingdom prepared
for you from the foundation of the world' (Matthew
25:34). To hear such words of welcome, when all
I deserve are words of condemnation, will be the
final proof of how much it mattered what I believed.

To pursue this subject:

*So What's the Difference? by Fritz Ridenour.
(Paperback, Gospel Light, Regal Books.)
**The Bible Tells us So, by R. B. Kuiper. (Paper-
back, The Banner of Truth Trust. The chapter
you have just read is based on chapter 10 of
this book.)
****A Christian Introduction to the Religions of the
World* by J. G. Vos. (Paperback, Baker Book
House.)

9.
Why do Christians have to be different?

One of the chief criticisms levelled at Christians is that they 'have to be different'. This is especially true at work. When certain social events are organized at the factory or office, the Christians are often nowhere to be seen. When the lunch-hour is over, and when almost everybody else is still finishing off their lunch-time drinks, the Christians are back at their desks on time. They do not tell the sort of jokes which are generally most popular, and disapprove of a great deal of commonly used language. What is wrong with them? Do they think they are a cut above other people? Why do they have to be like that?

Christians are 'mugs'. They declare all sources of income on their tax returns, pay the correct fare on the buses and tell the shopkeeper when they have been given too much change. They go to the police station with property they find in the street, and refuse to buy cheap goods which they suspect might have been stolen. They pay the higher fee for their TV licence on the very day they change from black-and-white to colour. When they drive they actually keep to the speed limit! Do these things really matter very much? Why is it that these people cannot be the same as everybody else?

Their homes are different, too. They spend more time with their children, expect them to be obedient and keep a check on what they watch on television. John does not 'go out with the boys', and Mary is never at the bingo. Most of their leisure time they

109

spend either together, or 'down at the church'. And
why can't they keep themselves to themselves, like
everybody else? What drives them to get so involved
with their neighbours, especially with the elderly?
Are they trying to be too good to be true? Why do
they have to be different?

Inwardly changed
The explantion for a Christian's different behaviour
is simple. He *is* different. He is not trying to be something which he is *not*. He is not striving to become
something else. Rather, a radical change has taken
place in his life, and his different behaviour is nothing
more than an expression of it. The change was an
inward one. Because his whole personality and outlook have been altered, it is inevitable that he will be
different from what he was before. He is a new
person, and we must not consider it unnatural for
him to live in a new way.

If you have read the previous chapters, it is
possible that you are under a misapprehension. We
have spoken a great deal about God's anger against
our sin, and our need of pardon. This is our first
and greatest need, and being put right with God is
the first blessing of the Christian life. But there is
more to it than that. Those who are put right with
God are also adopted into his family — a subject
which we do not have time to consider here. Not
only so, but the Holy Spirit enters them, and they
become *changed people*. Every true Christian is
indwelt by the Holy Spirit. There are no exceptions.
This is why Paul declared, 'If anyone does not have
the Spirit of Christ, he is not His' (Romans 8:9).
This means that they can never be the same again.
God is within them, and the progressive change which
he makes in their personalities is called *sanctification*.

Every man and woman who trusts in Christ has been inwardly renewed. When the prophet Ezekiel looked forward to the gospel age, he recorded the following promise from God for those times: 'And I shall give them one heart, and shall put a new spirit within them. And I shall take the heart of stone out of their flesh and give them a heart of flesh, that they may walk in My statutes and keep My ordinances, and do them. Then they will be My people, and I shall be their God' (Ezekiel 11:19—20).

From the moment of his conversion every true Christian has a burning desire to please God. A lack of this desire is an indication that the conversion has been spurious. The person imagines himself to have been converted when he has not. For the transformation in a genuine believer is so overwhelming that Paul has no hesitation in saying, 'If anyone is in Christ, he is a new creation; old things have passed away; behold, all things have become new' (2 Corinthians 5:17). Elsewhere the change is spoken of as a new birth, and the receiving of a new nature (1 Peter 1:23; 2 Peter 1:4). The Christian can never be the same again. 'You have put off the old man with his deeds', wrote Paul, 'and have put on the new man who is renewed in knowledge according to the image of Him who created him' (Colossians 3:10).

At conversion a Christian's whole nature is made new in a moment. This does not mean that he immediately becomes perfect. The new nature is like a new-born baby. It is complete from the beginning. But it needs to grow and to assert itself more and more against the sinful attitudes and habits which still remain in the believer's life, as left-overs from the days when he was a stranger to God.

A progressive change

The fact that he does not become perfect all at once is a source of continual distress to the Christian. In his heart of hearts he wants to please God. That is his constant and unchanging ambition. Yet each day finds him very different from what he most deeply wants to be. He says and does things which, deep down, he hates. He fails to live up to the standards of thought, speech and behaviour that he wants to keep. There is a constant gulf between what he wants to be and what he actually *is*. He longs for the resurrection day, when he will be all that he ever wanted to be, and repeatedly thanks God that future deliverance from his present distress is a certainty.

Every true Christian feels like this. He reads Paul's description of his own experience in Romans 7:7–25, and feels that Paul is writing about *him*. Other people may be indifferent to the sin which is in their lives, but it is against the whole nature of a Christian to be like them. They may be at peace with sin, but he is at war with it. They may dismiss their failures with a wave of the hand and say, 'Nobody's perfect,' but he cannot be so bland about it. He wants to be holy, and he is not.

Although he knows full well that he will not be perfect until the resurrection (Philippians 3:21; 1 John 3:2), the Christian does not give up the struggle against the things in his life which displease God. He does everything in his power to bring holiness to completion, never forgetting that he lives his life in God's presence (2 Corinthians 7:1). He longs for the sanctifying influence of the Holy Spirit to extend to every part of his personality (1 Thessalonians 5:23). His goal, of which he never loses sight, is that he may be like the Lord Jesus Christ (Romans 8:29; Philippians 1:9–11).

Most Christians are well aware that they are falling very short of likeness to Christ, and are slow to notice the progress they are making in holy thinking and living. However, from time to time a believer suddenly realizes that a sin which was an acute problem to him some time ago does not seriously trouble him any longer. He finds that he really *does* have power to say, 'No,' to it, just as God's Word had always assured him (see Romans chapters 6 and 7). He also finds that he progresses better in holy living by avoiding situations where he is likely to be tempted more strongly to sin than normal. He judges that it is better to avoid as much temptation as possible, rather than to face it and to fall. It is this deep-seated fear of sinning which causes many Christians to steer clear of places and practices of which others think nothing. Very often the thing concerned is not wrong *in itself*. But because the believer in question considers that he is more likely to sin there, he does not join in with those who go. It is not because he sees himself as a 'cut above' others that he stays away. It is the very opposite. He has a great sense of personal weakness. He knows that he should say, 'No,' to his old master of sin, but cannot always bring himself to do it. So he avoids him.

But he does not think only about his own weakness. He is part of a world-wide family of redeemed men and women, and their spiritual welfare is in his mind. He knows that there are many situations which he can enter without fear of sinning, with which another believer might not be able to cope. Let us take the issue of drinking alcohol. This is nowhere forbidden in the Bible, and is in no sense a sin. Our Lord drank alcohol when he was here on earth, and in fact his first miracle was to turn water into wine. Drunkenness is strongly forbidden by the Word of God and condemned in the boldest of terms. But not drinking alcohol.

This being so, why do so very many Christians totally abstain from it? They are free to enjoy it, but never touch it. This is because they all know fellow Christians, possibly members of the same church, who find it impossible to drink in moderation. Once faced with alcohol, they do not know when to stop. Soon they begin to lose control and may even become drunk. For them, the first drink is the certain road to sin. The caring Christian knows that his own example is an important factor in helping a fellow believer with such a weakness. He decides to show him that alcohol is not a necessity of life. The gospel is not about what you eat and drink, but it *is* about righteousness — not sinning. He therefore abstains from alcohol, and displays to the weaker Christian that he is not missing anything. You can get on very well without it.

Of course, those who are at work with the stronger Christian do not understand all this. When he refuses to go for a drink with them, they consider him to be anti-social. Nothing could be further from the truth. It is because he cares *deeply* for the welfare of others that he chooses to abstain. He *has* to be different — for the sake of his brother for whom Christ died.

Hard work — yet God's work
From all this it must be plain that the changes in a Christian's life do not just 'happen'. There is nothing automatic about them. The indwelling Holy Spirit has given him new affections and desires. His whole outlook has been changed and so, therefore, have his choices. But the Christian works hard at being

different, motivated by the indwelling God. Where this hard work is absent we have to conclude that the Holy Spirit is absent, too. The final proof that God is truly within him is the fact that he gives himself to the labour of living in a new way.

This is why the New Testament is filled with exhortations to Christians to live differently. If the changes in their lives just 'happened', such commands and encouragements would not be necessary. But believers are not puppets. The Spirit has given them a love for God's Word and they set themselves to obeying it.

They hear that they are expected to be holy: 'For this is the will of God, your sanctification . . . for God has not called us to uncleanness, but in holiness' (1 Thessalonians 4:3, 7). 'Be holy, for I am holy' (1 Peter 1:16). How can a child of God ignore such a command? The one who gives it is the one who has redeemed him by the death of his Son. Not only does the believer have a heartfelt love for God's Word, but sheer gratitude for all that God has done for him makes the thought of disobedience unthinkable. How can he engage in unholy talk and activity, when his God commands him otherwise?

Again and again the believer learns from the Scriptures that he is to throw off his sinful ways. It would be worth referring to your Bible again at this point and reading Ephesians 4:17—5:21. That is a very compact and comprehensive summary of the sort of behaviour that God expects from those who have come to know him. It does not contain only negative commands, but sets before the Christian positive aims. The chief of these is that they should be 'followers of God as dear children' (Ephesians 5:1).

A Christian cannot always remember precisely

what God expects of him in every situation. The
Bible is a large book, and his memory is weak. But
in every situation he can remember the command we
have just quoted. His life is to be patterned on the
character of his God. This character was exemplified
in Jesus Christ. He can ask in every situation, 'What
would Jesus do?' and then do the same. This is why
Paul wrote, 'Be followers of me, just as I also am of
Christ' (1 Corinthians 11:1), and 'Let this mind be
in you which was also in Christ Jesus . . .' (Philippians 2:5).

But from where does a Christian get the strength
to live differently? There is nothing easy about it,
especially when your friends mock you, and your
family misunderstands. We have already commented
on how weak we are. A Christian repeatedly wonders
how he can ever keep it up. But he does! How?

The answer is that God, by his indwelling Spirit,
gives supernatural strength to the believer. He could
never live the Christian life on his own. But the
Christian life is not lived in the strength of our own
resources. The mighty God within us supports us
throughout every step of our difficult journey.

There are some men and women who wait for a
feeling of strength before they set about seriously
obeying God. This is a serious mistake. Such people
in fact never feel the sense of strength for which
they are waiting, and come to nothing very quickly.

The true Christian does not wait to feel strong
before he begins a life of obedience. He obeys God,
not because he feels able to, but because it is *right*.
The moment he determines to obey, and actually
starts doing what he should, he finds that he *has*
the strength! This is God's way. As we work to live
in a way which pleases him, *he* works by his Spirit
within us, and gives us the support we need. We feel

too weak to do what he commands. But we walk by faith, and set about it, knowing full well that we can never do it on our own. We consider that we can do nothing else, because we love God's commands, and we love the God who gave them. His strength is seen in our weakness. As *we* work, *he* works in our lives, and we are able to do what he wants.

The moment we grasp this principle, a large number of verses in the New Testament suddenly make perfect sense. We now understand what Paul meant when he wrote, 'Therefore, my beloved, as you have always obeyed, not as in my presence only, but now much more in my absence, work out your own salvation with fear and trembling; for it is God who works in you both to will and to do for His good pleasure' (Philippians 2:12–13). It was as the Philippians *worked hard* at obeying the commands of Christ's apostle that God worked in them, and brought to pass his purpose of increasingly likening them to Christ. The proof that God was sanctifying them was that *they* did everything they could to live holy lives.

This is the way the Christian is progressively 'conformed to the image of His Son' (Romans 8:29), transformed 'from glory to glory' (2 Corinthians 3:18), 'renewed day by day' (2 Corinthians 4:16) and experiences the 'sanctification of the Spirit' (1 Peter 1:2). It is because all this is going on in his life that he is, inevitably, different.

The place of the Bible
It must now be obvious that no one can live a sanctified life who does not hear or read the Bible. You cannot obey a command of which you have not heard. You cannot set about doing what is pleasing to God if you do not know what it is. It is impossible

to live the life he requires if you are completely
ignorant of what he has said about it. The Bible and
holy living go hand in hand. The more a believer
exposes himself to God's Word, and obeys what he
hears and reads, the more like Christ he will be.

The Bible is God's chosen instrument for bringing
about sanctification in those who belong to him.
The psalmist wrote, 'How can a young man keep his
way pure? By keeping it according to Thy word'
(Psalm 119:9). Jesus prayed to his Father for his
people in this way, 'Sanctify them by Your truth.
Your word is truth' (John 17:17). But the most
comprehensive statement on this subject comes
from the apostle Paul's words to the young Timothy:
'All Scripture is given by inspiration of God, and is
profitable for doctrine, for reproof, for correction,
for instruction in righteousness, that the man of
God may be complete, thoroughly equipped for
every good work' (2 Timothy 3:16–17).

The Christian needs the Bible if he is to become
what God wants him to be. But, as that verse makes
plain, he does not need anything *in addition* to the
Bible. He can, by proper attention to its pages,
become all that God requires — both in knowledge
and in life. It is of paramount importance, therefore, that he should know *all* the Bible, and not
just a few favourite passages. Jesus underlined this
point when he said, 'Man shall not live by bread
alone, but by every word that proceeds out of the
mouth of God' (Matthew 4:4).

We live in an age when, in most Western countries at least, it is possible for almost everyone to
have a Bible of his own. This is an unfathomable
privilege! It was not like this in the earliest days
of the Christian church. Printing had not been
invented, and handwritten books were exorbitant

in price. Very often there was only one Bible for each congregation. Yet those early Christians knew their Bibles from end to end, and put to shame our modern ignorance. What was their secret?

They discovered the Bible *together*. We ‚‚ know that we get more out of a Bible passage ‚/hen we examine it with others. This is because Christ is pleased to display his presence to gathered groups of Christians in a way in which he does not display it when we are on our own (see Matthew 18:20). Individual Bible reading is a marvellous habit and should be encouraged everywhere. But a return to discovering the Bible together would enrich lots of Christians who are at the moment struggling.

That is not the whole of the early church's secret. Throughout history there have been men who have been gifted in understanding God's Word, and in explaining it to others. They have been able to see not only the meaning, but how it works out in practice. This ability is not a natural ability, or the result of having a superior intellect. These men receive this gift from Christ. They are *his* gifts to the church, so that we might all make spiritual progress and, in turn, discover our own spiritual gifts (see Ephesians 4:11—16). It is right that such men should form the leadership of the church, and should be supported by its gifts (1 Timothy 5:17). Listening to such gifted men is the very best way of getting to know God's Word, and therefore of becoming more holy in our lives. We need to give attention not only to what they say, but also to how we listen to them (Luke 8:18). The proper hearing of the Word of God is the most important single factor in making progress in the Christian life.

We need to note that private reading, studying together and listening to preaching are not the only

ways in which the lessons of God's Word are
impressed on our lives. When babies are small, their
parents do everything for them. As they grow older,
they are rightly expected to do more and more for
themselves. Often this is not easy. How many of us
have shed tears when left to dress ourselves or,
when older, when we had to make a journey on our
own? But these difficult experiences were an essential part of our progress from childhood to maturity.
The alternative would have been a state of perpetual
infancy. No loving parent could ever contemplate
leaving his child in such a state.

In exactly the same way God leads his children
through difficult experiences. None of them is
pleasant at the time, but all of them lead to a greater
degree of holy thinking and living (Hebrews 12:10—
11). These experiences are too diverse and numerous
for us to list. But we can mention some of them and
the effect they have on us.

Sometimes a believer has a period of doubt. He is
no longer sure that the Christian faith is true. Unlike
the unconverted person, such doubt does not lead
him to scoff, or to walk out on what he previously
believed. It moves him to search the Bible like never
before, and to examine its integrity in a new way.
How many of us have come to know parts of the
Bible which we hardly knew before during such a
search! This in turn advanced our Christian understanding and radically transformed our behaviour in
some areas. The difficult experience worked out for
our good!

Bereavement, pain and illness often make the
unbeliever bitter. They lead the believer to lean in a
new way on God's promises of comfort. Consequently his confidence in the truth of God's Word
and its relevance is considerably strengthened.

Perplexity leads him to claim God's promise to give him wisdom. Persecution moves him to re-examine Christ's example and helps him to walk more surely the path of forgiving others. Lengthy illness makes him see how very comforting the briefest visit can be, and gives him new thoughtfulness in this direction with friends and neighbours. Every hard experience brings him to learn a new lesson from God's Word, or to learn an old lesson in a new way.

The Holy Spirit is the true Author of Scripture, and is also the one who implants divine life in the heart of the Christian believer. Exposure to Scripture causes that divine life to manifest itself more strongly. Every activity of the Spirit leads the believer back to the pages of the Bible. As the years go by, the believer becomes increasingly a man or woman of the book. It rules his belief, affections, choices — and even his emotions. Spiritual influences become more and more dominant, until he is prepared to go to the Father's home, where all is holiness and where Christ is the sun and the centre.

The unbeliever knows nothing of this personal marriage to the Word of God. He may believe parts of it, and may even seek to obey some of its precepts. But he is not captivated and conquered by it, and very often prefers his own ideas to what it teaches. The Father of which it speaks is not someone *he* knows as Father. Its Christ is not his Lord. The Author of its pages is not the driving Spirit in his life. He does not rest on its promises and rejoice in what it unveils. It is not his comforting companion at the moment of his departing.

The difference between the unbeliever and the believer is immense. They are going in different directions and therefore going further apart by the minute. Unless the unbeliever turns round, the

separation will soon be eternal. The true believer is
not able to turn around and face the way that he did
before. The Holy Spirit impels him in a heavenly
direction. The glories of his future home appear
ever brighter and the attractions of this present world
recede every hour. Although everybody else seems to
be rushing past him in the opposite direction, he
cannot go with them. He *has* to be different.

To pursue this subject:

  Some Names Worth Having, by Francis W. Dixon.
  (Paperback, Lakeland-Marshall, Morgan and
  Scott.)
  **What in the world is a Christian?* by John Blan-
  chard. (Paperback, Evangelical Press.)
  ***God's Way of Holiness,* by Horatius Bonar.
  (Paperback, Evangelical Press.)

10.
What happens when we die?

Only the Bible can speak with authority about death. As we have seen earlier, death is not natural to the human race. It is an invasion into the way things were intended to be. This is why we fear it. It is God's judgement upon our wayward race. Because it was he who imposed it, he alone can tell us the truth about it. In this chapter we simply give a summary of what he has said about it in his Word.

'If only someone had come back from the dead to tell us what it is like!' is a wish we often hear expressed. People who talk like that have obviously forgotten Jesus Christ. The evidence for his resurrection is conclusive, as we saw in chapter 5. After his resurrection he spent forty days with his apostles. The apostle Paul was not a Christian at the time, but was personally taught by the risen Christ at a later date. The Spirit of Christ, working through the Old Testament writers, had already revealed a good deal about what happens after death. But the writings of the apostles in the New Testament are the clearest teachings on the subject which exist anywhere in the world.

Almost everything in this chapter is drawn directly from what the apostles wrote. The parts that are not are drawn directly from other parts of the Bible. We shall not encumber our pages with scores of Bible references, although we shall mention a few. Those who want chapter and verse for what is taught in this chapter should work through the simple but comprehensive book by William Hendriksen which is recommended at the end.

Death

At death we do not continue to be what we are now; but nor do we become what we shall be throughout eternity. It is, therefore, an *intermediate state* — an in-between stage, sandwiched by our present and final states.

We must remember that we are not just bodies, but that each one of us is body and spirit. When God made man, he formed his body from the ground. He was physically shaped, but was not at this stage *alive*. After this God breathed into him, 'and man became a living being' (Genesis 2:7). It was this union of the spirit which God imparted with the already existing body which made man *man*. There is both a physical and an invisible side to his make-up.

Death is the separation of body and spirit. It is the spirit which gives the body the indefinable quality of *life*. Once the spirit is gone, the body is no longer alive, and returns to the dust from which it was made. It decomposes and eventually all trace of it has disappeared.

But that is not the end of the *person*. It is the invisible side of each man or woman which is the real 'you', and this does not go out of existence at death. Throughout life the body is dying and being renewed. Virtually every cell in the human frame is replaced every seven years. By the time you have your twenty-first birthday you have been through three bodies! But you are essentially the same 'you'— albeit wiser and more mature. The real 'you' expresses itself by means of the body, but does not depend on the body for its existence.

So it is that when body and spirit are separated at death, the spirit continues without the body. Death is not the end. At the very moment of death the spirits of believers pass at once into the perfect enjoyment of the presence of Christ. Unbelievers begin their torment. The body may lie 'a-mouldering in the grave', but the real 'you' continues to be conscious. The Bible knows nothing of soul-sleep — the view that people are unconscious between death and the resurrection. Nor does it know anything of purgatory, or any other destination which is neither heaven nor hell. The moment of death marks the beginning of either our unspoiled enjoyment of Christ, or of our endless agony.

As far as the body is concerned, death is the same for both believers and unbelievers; but not as far as the spirit is concerned. The separation which began in life is now final. It is too late to repent and to believe the gospel and to enter into its eternal and priceless benefits.

We should not be misled by the fact that a Christian's body rots as easily as that of an unbeliever. The *whole person* matters to God, body as well as spirit. There is a future for the body. For the Christian it is a glorious future. The Bible says very little about the deceased bodies of unbelievers, but constantly assures believers that when Christ redeemed them, he purchased their bodies as well as their spirits. In the intermediate state the Christian feels 'naked' without a body and longs for the resurrection. This will take place at the end of the world, and his body will then be wonderfully transformed—to be like Christ's glorious body! (Philippians 3:20–21.) 'We shall be like Him, for we shall see Him as He is' (1 John 3:1–3).

What a hope to comfort and sustain a believer at the moment of death! Even Job, who lived without the full light of New Testament days, knew of this. 'As for me,' he said, 'I know that my Redeemer lives, and at the last He will take His stand on the earth. Even after my skin is flayed, yet from my flesh I shall see God; whom I myself shall behold, and whom my eyes shall see and not another' (Job 19:25—27 mg.).

The resurrection

What Job knew dimly, the New Testament declares plainly. You are not reading a manual on Christian doctrine, and we cannot here cover every detail. But the main points which the New Testament reveals about the resurrection are the ones which follow.

The *fact* of the resurrection is repeatedly underlined. The grave is not the final resting-place for anyone. Just and unjust alike will be raised from the dead on the last day. This seems incredible to men and women who are not believers, and they very often scoff at the idea. But this does not alter the fact. God has pledged to raise all who have ever lived and died.

The *manner* of the resurrection is revealed as far as believers are concerned. Nothing at all is said about the sort of bodies that unbelievers will have throughout eternity, apart from the fact that they will be capable of enduring eternal punishment without annihilation.

When a grain of wheat is put into the ground it eventually disappears. Instead there grows up a whole stalk of wheat. The grains in the head are similar to the one which was sown, and could not possibly exist unless the first grain had 'died'. There is a continuity between what was sown and what grows, and yet the plant which finally emerges is infinitely more glorious than the insignificant seed which was originally planted.

It is precisely this illustration which the New Testament uses to describe the resurrection of believers. The new body could not possibly exist unless there had first been the original body. There is a continuity of existence between the two. And yet the body to be is not the *same* body as the one which was buried. It is infinitely more glorious and has many new powers. It is like the body which Christ had after *his* resurrection, and yet is still very obviously the body of the person who died. The relation between this body and the next can be summarized in four words — *identity, continuity, dissimilarity* and *glory.*

The *certainty* of the resurrection rests upon the already accomplished resurrection of Christ. An important strand of New Testament teaching is that believers are united to Christ. The life he lived is reckoned to be *their* life — which is why they are seen as righteous in God's sight. The death that he died is reckoned to have been *their* death — which is why there is no punishment for sin for any of them to bear. In the same way, the resurrection of Christ is reckoned to be *their* resurrection. This is why they have already been raised from the dead spiritually, and enjoy spiritual life. Their physical resurrection is also assured. Christ did not rise just for himself, but for all who would believe in him. As he is, so they will be.

The *time* of the resurrection is the end of the world — 'the last day'. Events will take place in a certain order. When Christ comes again there will still be Christians alive on the earth. They will not enter into glory, body and spirit, ahead of those who have died. Dead Christians will be raised first, and their resurrected bodies will be incorruptible, and after a new pattern. Then Christians still in mortal bodies will have those bodies instantly changed into the same pattern. The mortal will

put on immortality. The resurrection of the unjust
will follow. All this will come about through the
invincible power of Christ. As at creation, he will
but speak the word, and it will be done. The whole
train of events will be the final proof of his deity
and lordship.

The *effect* that this teaching should have on our
present lives is also revealed in the New Testament.
When fellow believers die, we are naturally sorry.
But we should not grieve like people who have no
hope. Death is in no sense a tragedy for the Christian. The deceased believer is already with Christ,
and his body will eventually also take on Christ's
likeness. The fact that the body has a future should
move us to treat it with respect. Cremation can
obviously have no effect on the resurrection. None
the less it gives the impression that the body is an
object of little or no importance — and to encourage
that impression is wrong.

The thought of the resurrection should fill us
with hope and make us determine to live the whole
of our lives for God. Death is not the end, and we
should not live as if it were. Nor should we measure
a person's achievements by the effect their mortal
life has had on others. God's estimate is all that
matters — the God whom we shall all meet at the
last day. We should not be discouraged in Christian
work, but should give ourselves to it with unflagging
energy. Our work cannot be lost. It cannot come
to nothing. The final triumph lies in God's hands,
and that perspective should colour everything we
do.

A perplexing question

When we see how much the Bible speaks about the
resurrection of believers, it raises a perplexing

question in our minds. Why should Christians die in the first place? Is not death 'the wages of sin', and has not Christ borne the full penalty of sin? If all that we deserve has fallen upon *him*, why do we need to die? Has he not experienced it on our behalf already?

This is not a question which the Bible answers directly. Instead it seeks to comfort believers in the face of death by reminding them of certain truths. It assures us that death will one day lose *all* its power over the believer. Even now it has been robbed of its sting. We have a natural apprehension of it, and yet there is nothing unpleasant about it for the believer. It cannot hurt us or bring us any discomfort. The act of dying may be painful, but death itself is not to be feared. Like everything that God leads us through, it is for our good — even if our frail wisdom cannot see how. It cannot separate us from the love of God, and we can be certain of the Good Shepherd's strengthening presence when our turn comes.

If that was all the Bible said, it would be more than enough. But there is more. It teaches us that death is not something which happens at the *end* of life. The very day that Adam ate the forbidden fruit, he died. And yet he lived on the earth for centuries afterwards! The death which he died on the day of his disobedience was a spiritual death. His spirit was no longer in intimate fellowship with the Source of its being. He was out of touch with God, and out of his favour. He was set upon a course of sin. God's curse was upon him. The physical death which he died several hundred years later was but the logical consequence of the spiritual death which occurred on the day of the Fall.

Believers are already delivered from spiritual death. They are spiritually alive. They are restored to fellowship with God. They enjoy him in this life. The Bible calls this spiritual resurrection 'the first resurrection'.

But although they are delivered from the spiritual condition called death, believers are not yet delivered from the *physical* condition. They are not taken into God's immediate presence at the very moment they believe. But nor do they live here for ever and ever. They are born, live and die like other people. Believer and unbeliever live side by side in the world, and face the same ultimate reality. They rub shoulder to shoulder, even up to the very moment of death.

If all believers were snatched off to heaven the moment they believed, who would spread the gospel to other men and women? This is a task which God, in his wisdom, has not committed even to angels. It is those who themselves know the power of the gospel who must spread it. God's method of saving sinners is that they should hear the message proclaimed to them by human lips.

If believers lived on earth without dying, where would be the place of faith? Unbelievers would soon see that all who believed the gospel never died. They would be persuaded of the truth of the gospel *by the evidence of their senses.* This is not God's way. 'Without *faith* it is impossible to please Him, for he who comes to God must *believe* . . .' (Hebrews 11:6, italics mine).

Therefore although we do not understand all the reasons, as believers we should be content to live to God's glory, and then to die. We can rest on his unbreakable promise that we shall then be immediately with the Lord, and at last glorified in both body and spirit. We are not being asked to go along an untrodden path. It is the way the Saviour went. Why should we be afraid to follow?

The judgement

After death comes the judgement. One is as certain as the other. God has fixed the day and appointed the Judge! He has given us all assurance of this by raising him from the dead (Acts 17:31).

The judgement will take place at Christ's second coming. It will be preceded by the resurrection, and followed by the dissolution of the present universe. It will be the last great event experienced by the human race before we all enter the final condition in which we shall be throughout eternity.

Not only will nations be present at the judgement, but also every individual who has ever lived. No one will be left out, and nobody will escape. Besides the enormous throng of humanity, there will also be present the fallen angels who joined in Satan's rebellion. Every action will be considered by the Lord Jesus Christ, and also every word. Even our inmost thoughts and motives will be examined. It will be a time when every secret thing is made public. Nothing has ever been hidden from God, and that day will declare it.

It will be an awful day. Nothing done by any man or woman will be overlooked. Even the very springs which control us will be put on public view. It will be the day when the just God shows that he has been in all places at all times, and every action in the world's history has been done in his presence. It will be the day when we hear the words Christ spoke on earth bearing witness against all who rejected him. All will be found guilty, and all excuses will die on our lips. A terrified solemnity will take hold of us as we remember that 'It is a fearful thing to fall into the hands of the living God!' (Hebrews 10:31.)

And yet, despite all our evident guilt, no believers

will be condemned on that day! Christ will present us
as guiltless, and we will dance with wonder. The
record of our sins will be heard by all, and yet no
blame will be laid at our door. We shall be seen as
those who are at peace with God, and upon whom
none of his anger will fall. It will be revealed that
the entire punishment that our wickedness deserves
has fallen on the Lord Jesus Christ. The penalty has
been paid in full. It will be announced that his
perfect life was lived on our behalf, that it is
reckoned to our account, and that we are therefore
irreproachable in God's sight. 'For God has not
appointed us to wrath, but to obtain salvation by
our Lord Jesus Christ, who died for us, that whether
we wake or sleep, we should live together with
Him' (1 Thessalonians 5:9—10).

It is true that we will hear words addressed to us
from the throne, but there will be no note of condemnation in the voice which speaks. Rather, we
will be told that we are welcomed into glory. We
will be assured that the eternal dwelling-place of
God is our home, and that Christ has prepared
places for each one of us there. With unrestrained
happiness we shall proceed from the judgement seat
to our eternal habitation in the new heaven and the
new earth where 'there shall be no more death, nor
sorrow, nor crying; and there shall be no more pain,
for the former things have passed away' (Revelation
21:4).

The certainty of our glorious destiny should not
lead us to overlook that at the judgement our work
will be scrutinized. God will closely examine what
we have done for him in this life. He will test it
and, if it has been shoddy, we shall see him treat it
like the rubbish it is. 'The fire will test each one's
work, of what sort it is' (1 Corinthians 3:13). He

will not be looking at how much we have done, but at the *quality* of our workmanship. Did we do our best, or did we say, 'That'll do!'? Was there any skimping, or did we serve God to the limit of our ability? Did he have our finest hours, or the leftovers? Some will see God express disgust with what they did for him. How ashamed they will be! They themselves will be saved, but their work will come to nothing. On the other hand, those who engaged in costly and faithful service will be rewarded. It will have been worth serving Christ!

Eternity

What will happen to the unconverted at the judgement? For them the last day will be misery. Having never fled to the only Saviour of sinners, they will have to bear the penalty of their sins themselves. Their punishment will be terrible. Each offence against God is an offence against an infinite person. Each offence is therefore an infinite offence. Only an infinite punishment will be just for such sins.

It is not popular to talk about the eternal punishment of the unrepentant. But the Bible does not limit itself to what we want to hear. It tells us the truth even when that truth is desperately unpleasant. Its motive, however, is always the same. We are told of the coming and certain punishment of unbelievers so that we can repent and believe the gospel while there is still time.

The terms in which Scripture speaks of damnation are horrific. Paul says that the wicked will experience 'indignation and wrath, tribulation and anguish' (Romans 2:8–9). The Lord Jesus Christ will take 'vengeance on those who do not know God, and on those who do not obey the gospel of our Lord Jesus Christ. These will be punished with everlasting

destruction from the presence of the Lord and from
the glory of His power, when He comes, in that Day'
(2 Thessalonians 1:8—10). When John, in his vision,
saw the unrelieved misery of those who died without
faith in Christ, he could only describe the awfulness
of their place of punishment as 'the lake of fire'
(Revelation 20:11—15).

All of hell will be unspeakably terrible. But some
will suffer there more than others. Sodom was a
proverbially wicked city, but Jesus declared that the
inhabitants of Capernaum would be worse off at the
judgement than the Sodomites. The Son of God
himself had walked the streets of Capernaum and
performed amazing miracles there. If the people of
Sodom had seen such things, they would have
repented. The inhabitants of Capernaum were infinitely more hard-hearted. They were unmoved by
their great privileges and continued in their sin.

The Bible declares that those who have had the
most light will receive the worst punishment. God
expects more from those who have had greater privileges and opportunities. Those who have never heard
the gospel will fare better at the judgement than
those who have heard, but rejected it. The guilty who
had no access to a Bible will not be as severely
punished as those who possessed Bibles which they
never read — or read, but never heeded. Many people
in this world have never had any sort of contact with
a Christian. There are others who have been spoken
to again and again, but have not yet set themselves
to seek God. All of them await the penalty which
their sins deserve. But to sin against the light is
worse than sinning in ignorance.

Worst punished of all will be those who have been
convinced of the truth of the gospel, have made
some sort of claim to be a Christian, and have even

known something of the gospel's power in their lives — and then have walked out on it all. Such people do not only deliberately sin against the light. They bring shame on the gospel, and on the Son of God whom it presents. They bring the only saving message into contempt. They treat what they know to be good as evil. They treat the Saviour as an impostor. They give the impression that the gospel is nothing more than a human message which can effect no permanent change in men and women: 'For if we sin wilfully after we have received the knowledge of the truth, there no longer remains a sacrifice for sins, but a certain fearful expectation of judgement, and fiery indignation which will devour the adversaries' (Hebrews 10:26—27).

Now is the time
But we are not dead yet. The resurrection is still an event which lies in the future, and so is the judgement. As you read these pages you are neither in heaven nor hell. It is already too late for millions to repent and believe, but not for you. Your time has not yet run out, but who knows when it will?

> Seek the Lord while He may be found;
> Call upon Him while He is near.
> Let the wicked forsake his way,
> And the unrighteous man his thoughts;
> And let him return to the Lord,
> And He will have compassion on him;
> And to our God,
> For He will abundantly pardon
> (Isaiah 55:6—7).

To pursue this subject:

God's Light on Man's Destiny, by R. A. Finlayson. (Booklet, Knox Press, Edinburgh).

**The Bible on the Life Hereafter,* by William Hendriksen. (Paperback, distributed by Evangelical Press).

***Immortality,* by Loraine Boettner. (Hardback, Presbyterian and Reformed Publishing Company).

11.
How can I be sure?

Once a person has become a true Christian, he may know with absolute certainty that he is a child of God, that all his sins are pardoned, that he has passed from spiritual death to eternal life and that he is bound for heaven. In short, he may be sure that the Son of God loved him, and gave himself for him. He may go through life with *assurance.*

Some believers lack assurance

Yet it is a fact that many Christians lack this assurance. All their hopes of being accepted by God rest on Jesus Christ. But they have no sense of being at peace with God. They go through life filled with self-questioning and doubts. Their constant question is 'Am I a true Christian, or am I a counterfeit? Am I truly one of those who are accepted by God, or am I deceiving myself?'

Why should this be so?

One of the reasons is that many Christians look upon the very idea of assurance with suspicion. In their view, any claim to be absolutely sure of one's salvation is presumptuous. 'You must be a very shallow sort of person if you think like that! Surely no one who knows anything about the deceitfulness of the human heart can be so "cocksure". How often have we been "sure" of things which later proved not to be certain at all!'

Such people are not wrong about how easily misled the human heart can be. But they are completely wrong about assurance. The Bible makes it

137

perfectly plain that such assurance is the believer's normal experience. The believers mentioned on the pages of Scripture were not filled with self-questioning. They had plenty of emotional trouble. They were not strangers to sorrow. They had frequent cause to mourn over the sin which remained in their lives. They experienced opposition and adversity, and frequent heartbreak over the state of the church. But they did not doubt their own acceptance with God. They were confident of it. Why not take down your Bible again, and consider some of the passages which demonstrate this — for instance Romans 5:1—2, Galatians 2:20, 2 Timothy 4:7—8 and 1 John 3:14? It will quickly become evident that a believer was never intended to doubt that he is a child of God. It is not an experience he is expected to go through.

Some Christians lack assurance because they are put off by their failures and sins. They see their ungodliness, and lose their peace. 'If I was a true Christian,' they say, 'these things would simply not be found in my life. Can I really be a person who is indwelt by the Holy Spirit when I see so many examples of unholiness in my thoughts, words and deeds?'

If such people had a better understanding of what Christ did by his life, death and resurrection, they would not argue in this way. I must not think that I am more acceptable to God on the days that I live well, but less acceptable to him on the days that I fail and live badly. My own performance has never been the ground upon which God accepts me. Nor will it ever be. The life which I should have lived (but have not), *Christ* lived for me. That remains true, however I have lived today. The penalty I deserve for my sins was carried *completely* by

Christ, and so there is no penalty of any sort for me
to bear, today or any other day. This remains true
whether today was a 'success' or not. My daily
performance has no effect on my acceptance with
God. That rests entirely on what Christ has done
on my behalf. His work is over, has been accepted,
and will never be repeated. The benefit of what he
did was reckoned to my account the moment
I believed. As long as I rest on him, I have nothing
to fear — even when my faith is weak, defective
and shaken. It is not to strong believers, but to
believers plain and simple that the benefits of his
redemption flow.

> My love is oft-times low,
> My joy still ebbs and flows;
> But peace with Him remains the same —
> No change Jehovah knows.
>
> I change, He changes not,
> The Christ can never die;
> His love, not mine, the resting-place,
> His truth, not mine, the tie.

There is a third reason why some believers do not
have assurance. It is because they have a stereotyped
view of conversion. They hear others tell how they
came to Christ and, because their own experience
does not fit into the normal pattern, they doubt
whether their conversion has been real.

Such Christians need to recognize that no two
testimonies are the same. Some are awakened from
their spiritual death by a trumpet call — a dramatic
and traumatic experience. Others are awakened
gradually. Some are awakened as a mother awakens
a sleeping infant — with a kiss. In other words,

their experience is gentle, and its stages are not easily defined. The *manner* of awakening is not important. The real issue is whether a person has been awakened at all.

In all true conversions there are two elements. In all cases there is some consciousness of sin and of the need to be reconciled to God. There is also some grasp of the sufficiency of Christ to be the sinner's Saviour, by virtue of his life, death and resurrection. These two elements move the sinner to cast himself on Christ, and to find in him all his hopes of being accepted by God.

This does not mean that all believers have had a conviction of sin of the same intensity at the moment of their conversion. Some have not had the soul-shaking experiences which others have gone through. But they do not therefore need to doubt that their experience of conversion has been a true one. Were they sufficiently convinced of their sin to seek the mercy of God in Christ? That is the single point of importance. One's individual road to Christ does not matter. The destination is what is vital. Whatever road you have come by, do you have faith in the Lord Jesus Christ *now*?

If you have had a Christian upbringing it is particularly important that you should look at things in this way. You have been taught the truths of the gospel from your earliest years, and it is quite possible that you cannot recall precisely when you came to rest on Christ in a personal way. It may well have happened before your character was fully formed. Perhaps you cannot even remember a time when you did *not* love and trust him. The fact that you cannot pinpoint the exact moment of your conversion is of no importance whatever. Do not let the more easily definable experiences of others trouble

you. If, as you read this, you depend for your acceptance with God entirely upon the person and work of
the Lord Jesus Christ, you are a Christian indeed.
You need not let uncertainty spoil your joy for a
moment longer.

A fourth reason for lack of assurance is that some
Christians mix up 'faith' and 'strong faith'. Such
people see that their lives are not as 'saintly' as the
lives of others, and therefore wonder if they are
truly children of God. How close to God the other
person appears! How strong in faith and advanced
in knowledge! How mighty he is in prayer! What
zeal he has! What graces are seen in his life! When
we see such eminent men and women of God we
are very tempted to say, 'I am not in the same class
at all. My own spiritual life is so poor in comparison.
My life and his are a thousand miles apart. Perhaps
I do not have *any* spiritual life.'

This is quite the wrong conclusion to reach.
Certainly I am a poor specimen, but that does not
mean that I am not a Christian at all. My weakness
should grieve me. It should break my heart. But it
should not take away my assurance. It is true that
I am not what I should be. But it is equally true
that I am not what I used to be! I am a believer,
albeit an immature one. I am as nothing in Christian
stature when compared with others. But I derive all
my hope from the fact that God justifies the ungodly.
I rely for my acceptance with God, not on the
integrity of my Christian life, but on the finished
work of Christ on my behalf.

It is this reliance which marks out a true believer
from an unbeliever. No Christian can ever be perfect
in this life. There will always be room for improve-
ment. He will repent over his remaining deficiencies
every day. He will never be what he most deeply

wants to be. But his faith is in Christ and, for Christ's
sake, God accepts him. It is that fact alone which
makes his Christian life valid. It means that, however poor he may be when compared with others,
he need never doubt the certainty of his acceptance
with God.

Some people have false assurance

We have seen that some people who are entitled to
assurance do not have it. The opposite is also true.
There are some people who are *not* entitled to it
who *do* have it! They are sure that they are true
Christians, although they are not. They are self-
deceived. They have false assurance.

How does this awful situation arise? It is because
they are mistaken about what is the proof of being
a true believer. They accept certain things as
evidence, which the Bible flatly rejects. Because
they misunderstand what are the signs of being a
true Christian, they come to misguided conclusions
about their own standing with God.

Let us give some examples. In recent years there
has grown the widespread conviction that God is
restoring to the churches certain miraculous gifts
which have been absent since the days of the
apostles. Such gifts are held to include the power
to speak in tongues which have never been learned,
and the power to expel demons from those whose
personalities are controlled by them. Among those
who lay claim to these gifts are some who argue
that they could never possess them if they were
not true Christians. Does not their very enjoyment
of gifts given by the Holy Spirit prove that he is at
work in their lives?

It is beyond the purpose of this book to examine
whether these gifts are real or not. Let us assume

for the moment that they are. It still does not follow that those who possess them are true Christians. Judas had all the miraculous gifts which the other apostles enjoyed. But it turned out in the end that his spiritual experience was not genuine, and he was finally lost. Jesus himself predicted that many of those who will end up in hell will be those who, during their lifetime, exercised spiritual gifts in his name (Matthew 7:22). The possession of spiritual gifts tells us nothing about the person who has them. They are not proof of super spirituality, because they are not even proof of the most basic spiritual change of all.

We can give many other examples of a similar sort of reasoning. There are those who conclude that they are true Christians simply because they believe all that the Bible teaches. But it needs to be remembered that it is possible to know the Bible from end to end, and even to believe it, and not to know the power of its message in one's life. It is even possible, by the study of the Bible, to become an expert in all aspects of Christian experience, and to describe almost every situation and emotion which a genuine believer may go through — and yet not be a genuine believer oneself.

After all, although the Bible is not like any other book, it can be studied like any other book. Its contents can be mastered, tabulated, remembered and recited. All this can be done without the reader himself coming to repentance towards God and faith in our Lord Jesus Christ. Countless numbers of us knew exactly what was required of us years before we became Christians. We were in no sense strangers to the truth, but our faith was not yet resting in a *Person*!

Some, while reading or hearing the Bible, have

come under conviction of sin. They have realized in the most vivid manner that they are estranged from God, and under his wrath. Sometimes such conviction of sin has been of extraordinary intensity, and has lasted weeks and months. The experience has been almost infinitely traumatic.

Many who have had such an experience have concluded that they have been converted. But it is vital to realize that conviction of sin and conversion are not the same thing. There is more to conversion than seeing myself as a sinner. The realization must drive me to cast myself on Christ. If it does not, I cannot call myself a Christian, because I have neither repented nor believed.

On the other hand, if the conviction is not at all intense, but is none the less sufficient to move me to lay hold on the Saviour, it is enough. It is in fact quite common for believers to have had less devastating conviction of sin than those who never come to Christ. A few minutes' reflection will reveal why this is so. Their sense of sin makes them seek pardon. When they find it, their hearts are flooded with peace. But for the others there is no relief for their sense of guilt. Because they never seek pardon, it may go to an intensity never experienced by a believer. It may, as in the case of Judas, even drive them to suicide. They thus die in despair, and are ushered into eternity knowing nothing of what it means to be forgiven.

It is just the same with disillusionment with the world. There are tens of thousands of disappointed people on this planet. They have found no lasting happiness here. They are aware that all this world's joys are fleeting, and all that it promises comes to nothing. They feel that life is empty, and see themselves as alone. Very often they are filled with unabated pessimism and bitterness.

On the face of it, it may appear as if such people are Christians, or are very close to being so. Nothing could be further from the truth. There is more to being a Christian than discovering that this life is empty. The great feature of the believer is that he considers everything as worthless when compared with *Christ*. He will turn his back on everything else for the greater prize of knowing *him* (Philippians 3). It is because of the greater and eternal joys that he finds in Christ that he has such a low view of what the world offers. The new affection drives out the old. His life is thus the exact opposite of those who are disillusioned with the world. It is not one of unrelieved pessimism. The eyes of every believer are on the heavenly destination and the eternal home. It is in *that* light that this world is seen to be transient and unable to offer either solid joys or lasting treasure.

True assurance
False assurance is the result of mistaking what are the marks of a true Christian. How then does *true* assurance come? How may I discover whether I am a true believer, or whether I am deceiving myself?

The way to be sure is to examine both the New Testament and myself at the same time. The New Testament gives a clear picture of what a true Christian is like. With that in mind, I look at myself. Do I find that the New Testament picture, and what I see in my own life, are one and the same?

In other words, when I read the New Testament's description of a Christian, do I find that it is describing *me*? If so, there can be no doubt that I am a true child of God, and that any fears I have about my standing with God are groundless. But if the two pictures do not tally, it is evident that I am not a believer. It is time for me to repent of my sins, and to cast myself upon the mercy of God which is freely offered to me in his Son.

What *is* the picture which the New Testament gives of a true believer? First of all he is a person who has faith in the Lord Jesus Christ (Acts 20:21). This is something we learned about in chapter 6. A Christian has heard about Christ, and is convinced that he has heard the truth. He moves from this actually to put his trust in Christ. He makes an approach to him, and relies on the Lord Jesus Christ *as a person* to secure his acceptance with God.

The easiest way to discover whether I have such faith is to examine my prayers. I am God's creature, with a polluted nature and many actual sins of thought, word and deed. The eternal God is my Creator, and of purer eyes than to behold iniquity. Yet I pray to him, approach him and expect to be heard and received. On what basis? Why should *he* pay attention to *me*?

If I expect him to hear and receive me on the basis of the length or strength of my prayer, or on the basis of my good life, or my religion, or my intentions, or my church affiliation, or my need, or my weakness, or anything like that *whatever* — then I must face the fact that these are the things on which I truly rely for my acceptance with God. It is on them that my faith is placed, and I do not fit the picture of a New Testament believer.

When a true believer calls upon God he is painfully conscious of the awfulness of his sin, and remembers with relief that God's Son has died for sinners, and has borne their just penalty. All his hope of being heard rests on the fact that God justifies the ungodly, and that he reckons the righteousness of Christ to the account of all who come to him as Saviour. The true believer approaches God as a sinner. He is all too well aware that he should be excluded from heaven, but pleads the fact that there is one there who speaks on behalf of sinners, and guarantees their acceptance. If these considerations, and these considerations *alone*, are the basis of my expectancy of having access to God's throne, it is clear that my faith is in Christ. I have the first mark of a child of God.

The second distinguishing mark of a true Christian, according to the New Testament, is that he has a certain attitude to indwelling sin. What is my attitude to the plain fact that, even now, I do not keep the moral law of God? I have fallen short of his demands. I have even broken through his law by doing those things which he forbids. This is true of my outward actions, but also of my inward thoughts and motives. Do I greet this information with apathy? Is it only of slight interest to me? Do I yawn, and say that 'I have heard it all before'?

Or does the reminder trouble me? Does it sometimes break my heart, and cause me to cry out with inward despair? Am I ever bewildered by the fact that the things I do not want to do are the very things I do, and the things I want so much to do are too often the very duties in which I fail? Am I ever filled with dismay at the contradiction between what I *want* to be, and what in practice I actually *am*? Do I long — deeply and often — to be different?

It is in precisely such terms that Paul describes his own experience as a Christian in Romans 7: 14—25. This is how the heart of a child of God operates. We looked at this in chapter 9. Apathy to sin is the badge of the lost. Agony caused by indwelling sin is a marked feature of a true Christian. Is it a feature of me?

A third mark of a Christian is brotherly love. 'We know that we have passed from death to life, because we love the brethren' (1 John 3:14). How do we behave towards those that we love best? We consider their wishes, seek their welfare and are jealous for their reputation. We are willing to make almost any sacrifice to help them. We cannot keep them out of our thoughts for very long, and can hardly wait to be in their company again.

This is the way that true believers behave towards each other. They submit to one another, and seek each other's good. This love is not qualified or altered when the other person is unlovely, or temperamentally difficult. The bonds which unite Christians are bonds of mutual understanding and forgiveness. This applies however often the other has disappointed or offended me, or frustrated my plans and ambitions. My fellow believer is my *brother*. I will not be quick to judge him harshly, whatever provocations he may bring my way. We are members of the same family. The same blood has bought us. The same Spirit indwells us. We are bound for the same heavenly destination. We belong to one another, for time and for eternity.

It is true that I am bound to love my neighbour as myself. Christians are not the only people I must love. Yet my love for them is different. My attitudes and behaviour towards them betray my sense of oneness with them. If they do not, it is because I am *not* one of them. I do not have the third distinctive mark of a genuine believer. Anyone who is not burning with love for those whose faith is in Christ alone is misleading himself, if he thinks himself to be one of their number.

The work of the Spirit

It is by looking at these marks of a Christian which the New Testament provides that we are able to obey the command, 'Examine yourselves, whether you are in the faith' (2 Corinthians 13:5). Assurance comes through self-examination, and it is by the same process that false assurance is destroyed.

Yet there are passages in the New Testament which teach that our assurance is given to us by the Holy Spirit. For instance, Paul writes, 'The Spirit Himself bears witness with our spirit that we are children of God' (Romans 8:16, see also Galatians 4:6). What does that mean? And how does it fit in with our assertion that self-examination is the way to assurance?

To answer this we must remember that the Holy Spirit is the Author of the Scriptures. It was he who moved the human authors to pen what they wrote. This means that it is *he* who, ultimately, has provided the description of true believers which we have been examining.

Having himself given us these definite marks of a true Christian, it would be exceedingly strange if the Holy Spirit made no use of them in bringing us to assurance. The way that he works is this. We read in the Scriptures what a true believer looks like. After a little while we conclude that we are reading about *ourselves*. We say to ourselves, 'That description of a true Christian is a description of *me!*' The thought is borne in upon us with conviction. We are convinced that a general description in the Bible is actually descriptive of our own personal lives. We are entirely persuaded that we are the children of God being spoken about. Something written in cold print becomes to us heart-warming and reassuring. It becomes a source of daily strength and comfort.

What is the explanation of this? It is the work of the Holy Spirit. The divine Author uses the very Word he has inspired to bring assurance into the lives of those he has changed. He does not persuade us of our standing with God in a vacuum, but *by means* of the evidences which he himself has caused to be written in his Word. *This* is the way that the Holy Spirit convinces us that we are the children of God.

Assurance, then, does not come about by the Word alone. Nor does it come about by the Spirit alone. It comes about by the Holy Spirit working *through* the Word. It was by exactly this means that we were brought to Christ in the first place. All our spiritual convictions were born in our hearts by the same method. This is how the work of God proceeds in the human heart. His work of assurance is no departure from his normal way of working. How comforting to know that we may come to this happy position without special experiences!

We may expect, then, that the more a Christian is exposed to the Word which the Spirit uses, the more sure he will be of his standing with God. Conversely, we may expect assurance to decrease if the believer should ever neglect God's Word, or turn away from it. The experiences of Christians throughout the last two thousand years confirm this conclusion completely.

Nothing is more important to the Christian than exposure to God's Word. It is the food on which all spiritual life depends. Withdraw the food and the life will wither. But give it regular meals of faithful Bible preaching and daily Bible reading, and it is certain to prosper. The same course of action is to be recommended to those who are still not yet God's children. It is the best possible way of clearing up any questions which this book has not answered, but which you might have asked.

To pursue this subject:

Today's Gospel — Authentic or Synthetic? by Walter J. Chantry. (Paperback, The Banner of Truth Trust.)
**Knowing God,* by J. I. Packer. (Paperback, Hodder and Stoughton.)
***Add to Your Faith,* by Sinclair B. Ferguson. (Paperback, Pickering and Inglis.)

For details of a helpful system of daily Bible readings, write to:

Bible Study Notes,
7 Fleming Square,
Maryport,
Cumbria,
England.

Many thanks!

— to Inter-Varsity Press for kind permission to lean very heavily on chapters 2—4 of *Basic Christianity*, by John R. W. Stott, in the preparation of chapter 5. Mr Stott is Rector Emeritus of All Souls Church, Langham Place, London, and his book is available world-wide, in many different languages.

— to the Rev. Professor Donald McLeod, Professor of Systematic Theology at the Free Church College, Edinburgh, for kind permission to lean equally heavily on his two articles on *Christian Assurance* published in *The Banner of Truth* in October and November 1974, in the preparation of chapter 11.

— to The Banner of Truth Trust, Edinburgh, for their kind permission to use freely any of their publications in my writing. Chapter 8 of this book is closely based on chapter 10 of their publication *The Bible Tells us So* by R. B. Kuiper.